The One New Thing Project

My Mission to Get Unstuck, Break Through, and Hustle Joy

By Ann Bingham

Copyright © Ann Bingham

All rights reserved. No part of this book may be reproduced in any form or by any electronic or mechanical means, including information storage and retrieval systems, without permission in writing from the publisher, except by reviewers, who may quote brief passages in a review.

ISBN 978-0-9975042-7-9
Library of Congress Control Number 2021912394
Printed and bound in the United States of America
First Printing August 2021
Editing, book cover design, and interior formatting by:
Dean Diaries Publishing

To order additional copies of this book, contact the author:
Ann Bingham
hello@annbingham.com
www.theonenewthingproject.com

Table of Contents

Dedication v

Introduction 1

CHAPTER 1
    In The Beginning 7

CHAPTER 2
    Now For The Rest Of The Story 23

CHAPTER 3
    The Rules Of The Game 39

CHAPTER 4
    Big Things And Small Things 55

CHAPTER 5
    The Importance Of Grounding 73

CHAPTER 6
    Hobbies And Neverending New Things 93

CHAPTER 7
    How To Properly Fail 107

CHAPTER 8
    Shaking It Off 137

CHAPTER 9
    Getting Creative 153

CHAPTER 10
    Finding Your Joy 171

CHAPTER 11
    Passing It On 193

EPILOGUE
    One New Thing #287: Wrote a Book 213

Dedication

This book is dedicated to my big, weird, and wonderful family. Rob, Alex, Ryan, DJ, Stephanie, Matthew, and Kellie.

You all are my heart and soul.

Always remember to make stories.

Introduction

When my daughter, Alex, was in college, she wrote an article for the Odyssey Online entitled, "*11 Struggles of Having Parents Who Are Way Cooler than You.*" To be fair, my daughter was pretty stellar in her own right, as you'll learn. She wrote that piece a few years after I had started the One New Thing Project. Unbeknownst to me, she was experiencing changes right along with me. Our whole family was.

The One New Thing Project isn't just about making you cooler for your teenage kids. This started for me as a weird form of self-care. I always had a hard time getting on board with massages and manicures. They always seemed like such a great idea at the time, but I had to schedule time for them. They weren't cheap. With a demanding job and a busy life, I honestly couldn't imagine fitting things like that in on a regular basis. I mean, how do you tell your son, "No, I'm not coming to watch you play hockey. Mom's getting a massage instead?" Manicures and massage types of self-care always seemed so frivolous to me. Within 15 minutes of leaving a massage therapist, I had knots in my shoulders from traffic. Within days of getting my nails done, they were chipped and broken from washing my hands repeatedly at the preschool where I taught. It just wasn't worth the time and effort.

Introduction

Now, I know reading that, it's a lot like saying why bother making your bed if it's going to get slept in a few hours later? Self-care is an essential thing for all of us. The unfortunate reality is that many of us take this approach. It comes after kids' baths, after dinner, after everyone else has their new clothes and shoes. After everything.

I needed a way to make self-care happen during my life. To find joy again, without disturbing the fabric of my life. That's the simple story of how the One New Thing Project came about. Try a new thing a month. Just one. For one year, and that one year became almost ten.

What happened between #1 - my first taste of Mooncake, and #287 - wrote a book, truly unexpected. It's been far beyond new recipes, hobbies, and places visited. It's new friends, better relationships, more laughter, and so many more shared stories. Beyond that, it's meant a profound sense of who I am in this world. I'm surrounded by the people I care about and who care about me.

As I wrote this book from my home in South St. Louis during the summer of 2020, I was profoundly aware of two things. One, how fortunate I am for my place in this world. I have had many challenges in my life. I am deeply grateful for the people who have helped me through those times. I'm very aware that I have more than many people—more access, more resources, more of many things. My city, my state, is continuing

Introduction

to reckon with this long history of inequality. I have tried hard to keep this at the forefront of my writing, knowing that I likely have not always been successful. One of the founding tenants of the One New Thing Project is that it must be accessible to all, regardless of the time, money, and other resources you have available. This project is yours. Play with it.

2020 highlighted the need to take our health and self-care seriously. It also showed how distinctly difficult it is to do that when you have so many competing realities. Suddenly, the lines between our work, parenting, schooling, and relationships became an even bigger jumbled mess. What little was left in reserve to take care of ourselves seemed to dry up overnight. It feels right to say we have to care for ourselves first to have fuel in the tank to care for everyone else. Especially when there are babies in arms, kids that need help with online school, relationships to nurture, and rent to figure out. We know that's true, but it's just not that easy when the rubber hits the road. I hope the One New Thing Project helps you to untangle those lines just a bit. I hope that you're able to find one or two things to do with the people you care most about and some things that are just for you. It's been a hell of a year, and all of you deserve it.

My One New Thing Project journey started as a solitary one, but it ended up as a group adventure. I'm not sure that you

Introduction

can do anything that changes you so much entirely by yourself. There are always people who believe in you more than you do, building roads for you to walk on and constantly giving you supplies during the most challenging times. I know that for me, that was undoubtedly true.

Many people came along for this magical ride, and with whom I share many memories, laughs, and tears. My husband Rob, who's been with me for more new things than I can count, far before this project ever started. You're the love of my life. You've been my staunch supporter, my editor, and the officemate who has tolerated me yelling at my computer. My two kids Alex and Ryan--who made parenting an adventure. You two are who I want to be when I grow up.

Stephanie and D.J., I can't say how much I love both of you. There's an unspoken language that happens when you share as many things as we have. I treasure the two of you more than you can possibly know. Kathy and Holly - who were my very first one new thing partners. We shared so many laughs and maybe more tears. You will forever be my sisters.

Misty, even though you're across the state, you somehow let me talk you into running multiple half marathons and paid me back with subterranean paintball. Touché.

Alison, you are my ride or die. You remind me that I can do hard things--always. Colette, you know all of the good stories. Dave and his better half, Jenn, who is the biggest badass you'll ever meet. We've shared many new things with you—a memorable election night, beer fests, and the introduction to cool people/nerdom with my first Dungeons and Dragons.

To all of the women in the One New Thing Group—you are ambitious, adventurous, amazing people. Don't let anyone tell you differently.

And to you, good reader, for taking a big step into the cool unknown. Here's to you. Go make some stories.

Introduction

IN THE BEGINNING

HAVE YOU EVER SEEN THE WAY a three-year-old looks at bubbles? At a dump truck? At anything? There's awe. There's a wonder. There are squeals of delight. God, I miss that.

That's how this whole thing started: I was jealous of three-year-olds. While I'm not super proud to admit that, on the other hand, it led to a big experiment that would ultimately change my life. But let's not get ahead of ourselves here.

When our story begins, I was living a great but unassuming life. I was the director of a prominent preschool in St. Louis, Missouri. I worked with kids my entire life, which was my dream job - the one I wanted to retire from. We were connected with a high-profile university, so no expense was spared to attract top faculty and researchers to bring their burgeoning little geniuses to us. The building was state of the art—an eco-friendly facility that would make its own energy within a few years. Our building was designed to be completely recyclable, down to the bright yellow, orange, and purple flooring, which was a high-end product made of yeast and flour. There was a running joke that in a pinch, we could eat it.

Our school was designed for children to experience their environment fully and completely—floor-to-ceiling windows, three playgrounds, a school garden, and a nature trail that was created to draw in butterflies, grasshoppers, finches, and hummingbirds. We also had an indoor gym, an art studio, and a science lab—all with their separate teachers. I was on a first-name basis with the Chancellor of the university. Many of the more formidable faculty and administrators would often stop by to rock babies or play on our playground. Great facilities, great teachers, great families, and great support. This was absolutely everything I could have dreamt of. My Facebook posts were full of how much I loved my job, loved my coworkers, loved everything about what I was doing.

It was a long way from where I started my career when I was 16, being paid $3.25 an hour working after school in a childcare program 25 minutes from my house. Now I was almost 40. I had been recruited to open this school, leaving behind another program when I recognized what a fantastic opportunity this was. That first childcare job, like the one being a cashier at Walgreens, and all the other after-school attempts to earn money, didn't seem like it would be all that life-changing. It was a fun way to spend a couple of hours, get paid, and still get home in time to hang out with my friends. For a 16-year-old, that was after-school job gold. Twenty-odd years later, I still loved the smell of playdough.

So yes, I had a fabulous job that I loved. I also had a truly remarkable home life. It's embarrassing to say that I was starving for the joy that comes naturally to little kids when I had the dream life for all intents and purposes. I lived in a lovely two-story house in the suburbs—although to say that it was rarely clean is a vast understatement. I never understood how people managed what my mom called "the immaculate mother." My house was perpetually dusty, cluttered, and full of laundry, not to mention the funk from sports equipment. So much sports equipment. I might be getting it now.

While our house was never clean, it was always full. My husband Rob and I had been married almost 20 years at the time our story starts—one of those obnoxiously happy, made-for-TV relationships. You know the kind where there's just enough banter to keep it interesting, but not enough that you think *Geez, Ross and Rachel, spare us already.* Enough hand-holding and affection, but not so much that there's baby talk, and enough wanting to spend time together without it being like Silence of the Lambs.

Our family included two teenage kids—our daughter Alex, 15, and Ryan, two years younger. We lived in our house our kids' entire lives, which meant lots and lots of friends. Alex was a gifted student, musician, and athlete. She was always in one club, team, play, or orchestra, or another. And that meant for her friends to see her, they landed at our house. Ryan had what was once called Asperger's and started playing hockey around seven. Most of his friends (except one he made in Tiger Cubs in kindergarten) came from hockey. Ryan's friends have remained the same throughout his life. They got him, and the things that went along with his Autism weren't such a big deal. Ryan craved order so strongly, he didn't care to spend the night at anyone else's house where the food, bed, or routine might be different. His friends understood, and their parents were happy to not have a brood of boys crashing at their house staying up all night. That meant that in addition to Alex's friends, Ryan's friends also crashed at our house pretty frequently through high school.

I'm starting to get why I never achieved Immaculate Mother status.

And then there were my friends. Since Alex and Ryan kept the same friends most of their lives, the parents of those friends became our friends. Bonds were formed slowly but surely over wine planning Girl Scout and Tiger Cub meetings, sharing hot chocolate, cheering each other's kids on in cold ice rinks, and giggling through first-grade pageants. These women became my real housewives' sisters without the Botox and collagen. They were the kind of friends that were always there when you called and never questioned it. They just asked if you needed wine or a tarp and shovel.

We got each other through everything. We got each other through the *I hate my husband* moments, the *I'm moving to the beach* moments, the rebellious teen moments, and the dreaded freshman biology.

Freshman biology at our kids' high school had one of those teachers that you just endured. The class culminated with a semester-long plant growing experiment. Essentially, if your plant died, you failed. The paper that went along with it was roughly 20 pages long, listing in excruciating detail how plants were cared for, fed, watered, given sunlight sung to over 90 odd days of school, including spring break. Many plants died. Many kids got failing grades, leading to much crying, hyperventilating, and ultimately teenage fantasies about revenge against said biology teacher. In those 20 pages, the teacher required that students give an "honest review" of their experience. On the surface, this section was supposed to help the students with critical thinking while providing helpful information to improve the project in the future.

Alex was no dummy. She knew how to play this game. She objectively wrote about what she had learned, interspersing a bland compliment for the teacher here and there, and made a few suggestions. The teacher still uses Alex's paper as a model for students in her class to this day, ten years later. Ryan took the "honest review" at its word. He started his review section with, "This is the stupidest thing I've ever done." His review became more critical from there, citing case study on why students shouldn't be held liable for dead plants out of their control over spring break. How the workload of this paper far outweighed what should be expected for a freshman biology class for the weight of the grade assigned. In his opinion, the project and its paper were on par with college classes. Since he had taken a college class at a gifted academy the previous summer, he had a frame of reference. When I read it, I banged my head on the table. Tact, Ryan. Tact.

I expected to be called in to meet with the teacher for that section, but that's not what happened. The teacher responded with what I can only describe as an explosion of red ink. She circled comments, drew long arrows around his critique, and finally wrote on the last page, in bold, capital letters, WHO DO YOU THINK YOU ARE? "But she wanted an honest opinion to make it better. I gave her an honest opinion." I talked to Ryan until I had visions of steam pouring out of my ears. And that's when my friend, Kathy, stepped in. Because that's what good friends do. Sometimes they understand your kid better than you do. "Ryan, it's not about what she asked you to do. She asked for an honest opinion. But you needed to give it to her in a way that she could hear it. Does she strike you as the kind of person that would listen to that kind of criticism?" Kathy fixed my kid, and then she fixed me. We went out for a girls' night so that I didn't buy that ticket to the beach. Because that's what good friends do.

Our life was this way for a long time. Great job. Great life. Great marriage. Great kids. Great friends. Lots of laughter.

Do you ever notice people who post those "we're the happiest couples ever" posts end up with massive fights? Never. Ever. Trust them. At this point, you should be waiting for the other shoe to drop. Mostly because I started this chapter admitting that I was jealous of the joy of three-year-olds. Also, because in the back of my mind, something had begun to creep in. A word that I had read in lit books in high school but never got the true sense of it. Malaise.

Malaise. It's a good word. A quark word—one of those you study on your SATs, read in fancy literature, maybe on word-of-the-day toilet paper. It doesn't exactly come up in day-to-day conversation. Now it was a word that I found floating in my head like a marshy bog—one of those places that you wouldn't be caught dead in, slow-moving and smelly, but with a sense of intrigue about what lurked under its murky depths. Malaise.

It's a feeling of discomfort. Uneasiness. That feeling that you can't put words to but pervades everything. Not unhappiness, I was not that. Not angry. I was not that. I was malaise. The very obvious problem with malaise is that it is difficult to identify. You have this feeling that everyone else just sort of naturally gets the whole mom, wife, and working person thing. While you might be doing a bang-up job, you're doing it in a way that looks just a little off. Your square peg is kind of chafing in the round hole. Everyone else's house is clean, and you can't manage a Swiffer. Everyone else has orange slices for the team, and you're looking for Bailey's for your hot chocolate. Everyone else has one of five haircuts that come out of the salon, and you're secretly craving an extra ear piercing and purple hair. You're just left with this feeling that you have this fabulous life that you're sort of watching from a distance—appreciating, like a beautiful piece of art.

I kept those feelings to myself for a very long time. I tried hard to find an explanation—any explanation—depression? That didn't make sense. Midlife crisis? Maybe, but that seemed so cliché. And I wasn't looking to leave my husband and kids. I was truly happy with everything in my life. What I was…was searching. I just had no idea what I was searching for. I felt utterly alone.

Then suddenly, I wasn't.

Kathy and I often found escape from our busy households in a tiny Mexican restaurant close to our houses. One of the best things about La Chata was that it was within walking distance when things got too nuts at home. The brother and sister owners, Luis and Leticia, would greet you with a hug and no questions. Carefully sizing up your predicament, Luis would find the perfect tequila from his carefully crafted collection. Leticia would settle you at a quiet table with generous portions of her family recipes.

One night, as we sat eating homemade chips and salsa and sipping margaritas, Kathy asked me, "Do you ever wonder if this is all there is? I mean, I'm happy. I'm *really* happy…it's just…I kind of think I have everything I want right now. And like, what's next?"

I took a deep breath, and I ran my finger over the stem of my margarita glass. Someone else felt this way too. I wasn't alone. Kathy was staring into her half-empty glass. I suspect that she felt the same creeping guilt that I had, but she had the courage to say what I couldn't. Neither of us made eye contact for a moment. I finally laughed and said, "I'm so relieved it's not just me."

At that moment, I exhaled. I wasn't alone. At least one other human felt the same way I did, which meant I wasn't completely crazy. And that felt amazing. If I was having a midlife crisis, at least we were in it together. Knowing that I wasn't alone didn't stop the guilt. I was living a privileged life, and I knew it. I hadn't always had a life like this. I'd venture to say that most people still don't. I was deeply grateful for every bit of it. I was happy. (If you're envisioning me walking around with a giant grin that made my cheeks hurt, you're not far off.) At the same time, I was still searching. It was like taking a long road trip to Orlando and then hanging out at your super nice, rented vacation house with a pool. The house and pool are fabulous, but *are we doing anything else?*

After that conversation over margaritas, a singular thought kept hanging on, somewhere in the back of my head-- taunting me. There's more.

I had spent so much of my life in dogged pursuit of this exact moment--reaching, growing, achieving--that no one ever told me what to do when I got here. It's a lot like climbing a mountain. You get to the top and think, this is a great view, but the whole point was to climb the mountain. I built a cabin there. And more importantly, *I stayed inside.*

And then, one day, I found myself visiting a group of three-year-olds on the playground. I visited classrooms every day, so this wasn't such an unusual experience. It was a warm

September day, and the teachers had brought out shaving cream to play with. The playground is such a joyful place. Kids are free to run and explore, become astronauts, run with wild abandon, and chase grasshoppers. From the corner, I suddenly heard gales of laughter. A couple of kids had found the shaving cream and were enjoying squishing it between their chubby little fingers. One little boy slapped shaving cream between his hands, sending splatters of foam high into the air to the uproarious laughter of every child within ten feet. Over and over again. Slap. Foam. Gales of laughter. Pure, unadulterated exuberance. I wanted it. Every bit of it. The foam. The laughter. The joy.

  I joined in, slapping shaving cream, and it was fun. But to be honest, I was a forty-year-old woman, and my joy came from ten three-year-olds nearly falling over from laughing so hard. I didn't have that same unbridled joy. Damned kids. I wanted what they had. That exact feeling of finding something so amazing for the first time that it brings you to that kind of unbridled joy. I couldn't remember the last time I felt that. At that moment, I was envious of them—that pure, I don't care who's looking, or if you think it's stupid, I'm going to do this a thousand times because it's freaking amazing joy. That kind of joy. I wanted that.

  And that's when it started to form. Slowly, over a few days. An idea that began to take shape in the back of my mind clearing the fog of the malaise. Joy. That's what I was lacking. I was happy, but I didn't have joy. Somewhere between all of the great adulting I'd been doing that made me very happy, I had lost the joy. What would happen if I found that and kept the happy part? What if I could find real, true three-year-old joy again?

There's a difference between happiness and joy. It's subtle, but it's there if you look. Joy comes from some untapped well in your soul, at risk of bubbling over at any time. It's completely internal. But more importantly, it's a state that can evolve and be built upon throughout a lifetime. Happiness is dependent on external factors. It's based on other people, places, and things. It's keeping up with the Joneses. It's what's next. I was indeed caught up in happiness. I had "achieved," so now what? But those three-year-olds? They were just joyful because they just...well...were. It didn't matter if they had shaving cream, or paint, or a cardboard box. Their exuberance was infectious.

I made it my mission to find that three-year-old joy again. I spent as much time with them as I could. I looked at everything through their eyes, even food. Let's face it, broccoli isn't a kid's favorite side dish, but our chef managed to make it a little more tolerable. Our rule was everyone had to take a "Try It Bite." That meant me too, when I had lunch with the kids, and I despised broccoli. But I did it. One bite to try something new. That would prove to be the start of this adventure and the key to many other new things in the future.

I was a few months into my joy-seeking when I walked into the school staff lounge and found an ornately wrapped box that had been shipped from Singapore. It sat on the table unopened and ignored. A number of our teachers sat nearby and glanced at the box skeptically. Because our preschool was connected with a distinguished university doing a lot of groundbreaking research, we were fortunate to have families from all over the world attending our program. That meant that we were treated to culture, language, and cuisine from the farthest corners of the globe. We got many tasty treats, but this beautiful box of three small ornate Mooncakes remained untouched. Maybe it was the fact that it wasn't made by one of our families but had instead been sent by a fancy hotel in

Singapore. Perhaps it was the fact that no one exactly knew what was in Mooncake. I'm not entirely sure why they weren't touched, but I remembered that rule about the Try It Bite. So I opened the box and read the note. "In honor of the Malaysian Moon Festival. With Love, Grandma J." It was sent by the grandmother of one of our two-year-olds. She was a hospital administrator in Malaysia and occasionally flew in to spend a month with her grandson, spending almost every day volunteering in his classroom. She had become family to us.

At that moment, I decided to reclaim my three-year-old joy. The Mooncakes were about four or five inches in diameter. They had a sweet, somewhat sticky crust with an ornate pattern pressed into the top. They smelled slightly of honey and sesame and something I couldn't place. I cut a small piece, my Try It Bite. The inside had two fillings, one wrapped in the other. The outer one was a brownish and flowery, fragrant scent. The inner one had a familiar scent to it. I touched the tip of my tongue to the filling. It was sweet. The yellowy inner filling tasted a bit like custard. I took a small bite. It was delicious. My mouth was flooded with flavor—a sweet, floral flavor that I would later learn was lotus paste.

With one Try It Bite, a lifelong adventure was born. This was it. For a brief moment of lotus paste amazingness, I had that joy. It was remarkable how this small thing, this new thing, had brought about such a reaction in me—such utter delight.

In The Beginning

For a solid day, I was the Mooncake ambassador. "Oh my gosh! Have you tried the Mooncakes? They are amazing!" This was the thing, or more specifically, this was the kind of thing that I wanted more of. More new things.

So that's what I set out to do. I decided to do one new thing each month through the rest of that year and the following year. It would be my New Year's resolution—just starting a little early. I'd never finished a New Year's resolution, so this was going to be a big test for me. My record for the shortest resolution was to stop cursing, which lasted 14 seconds. I'm not good at goals and even worse at follow-through, so my friends kind of nodded kindly when I announced this one in September. To keep me honest, I promised to post my new things on Facebook. One new thing each and every month for 15 months, starting with the Mooncakes. That was the goal. Bring on the joy.

And I did. Mooncakes became getting a different kind of pet, became hacking a secret family recipe, and became belly dancing. I did finish that first year of new things, completing my first-ever New Year's Resolution (much to my friends' surprise). Somewhere in those first 15 months, it became more than a New Year's Resolution, and the One New Thing Project came to life. It became something woven into the fabric of my life that would have rippling effects far beyond different cuisines, new dance

In The Beginning

moves, and interesting pets. In the nine years since my first Try It Bite of those incredible mooncakes, the One New Thing Project evolved into well over 250 new things, often more than once a month. It became something to hold onto when life felt out of control and something that paved the way for an entirely new life that was on the way.

NOW FOR THE REST OF THE STORY

HERE'S THE THING ABOUT TRYING to keep something from your family. You can't. At least, I can't. So the whole time I was going through my life trying to figure out why I didn't feel like I completely fitted in, I was convinced that I was the only one feeling like something was off. Alex recently said to me, "You know, you thought we were always happy back then, we weren't." I was shocked that my well-crafted façade was not successful. Let that be a lesson to you, gentle reader. No matter how hard you try to hide the tough stuff, no matter how hard you try to round out the hard edges, kids will sniff it out like a fart in class.

It's still not easy for me to talk about difficult things in my life. And the time surrounding the One New Thing Project had many. During those times, there were unpleasant tasks that just had to be done, funerals to plan, jobs to leave, and many doctors to meet with. It was easier to just do what needed to be done and move on to the next thing—one more task checked off in an ongoing stream of bad things that I tried to keep to myself to keep away from my family. Again, bad idea. When one of you suffers, you all suffer.

Just before the One New Thing Project came along, I had three devastating losses in a row—my dad, my grandmother, and on the heels of her death, my mom. And suddenly, I felt incredibly alone in the world—completely untethered.

Growing up, our house was a quiet one. My parents didn't talk much, and they interacted with my brother and me separately. My dad used to love to take us to see Christmas lights at the Anheuser Busch Brewery when we were little. Mom would make my dresses. As I got older, they both got more distant, and their relationship grew noticeably strained. By the time I graduated from high school, they weren't talking to each other, and they weren't talking to me much. Our house became a tense place where my dad watched TV and drank beer in the living room. My mom sat at the kitchen table reading a dog-eared paperback while sipping iced tea.

My parents divorced in my senior year of high school. They had only spoken on a couple of occasions since—the first being our wedding and the second being the birth of their first grandchild, Alex. I became very close to both of my parents as I watched them embrace the role of grandparents, each decidedly different, but each in magical ways.

Dad would often drive the hour to our house, getting up well before dawn, to surprise our kids with chocolate milk and McDonald's before school. He was the grandpa who would show up at our house, ushering us out for dinner and a movie so that he could babysit. He bribed guys on the Walmart truck to get the *"ungettable"* toys for our kids for Christmas. If you never got Tickle Me, Elmo, that was my dad's fault.

Mom was all about experiences with the kids—squishing their toes in the mud. She lived with my grandmother, and she felt it was her job to show our kids our family's traditions. She taught them to bake and let them explore the treats in her garden. They would eat petit strawberries and munch on fresh mint and lemongrass. One of their favorite delicacies was something called Ranger Cookies. Ranger Cookies have a simple sugar cookie base, but it's all improvisation from there. It literally means if something is within range, it can go in the cookie. We've had lavender cookies and strawberry cream cookies, but we've also had cookies with Chex and Doritos. My grandmother would stand in the kitchen doorway and laugh at the assembly of the cookies—flour on every surface, as Alex and Ryan stirred in their unique combination. My grandma would try to interject some sort of common sense, "I'm not sure that's going to taste very good, Pat." My mom, completely unfazed, would continue helping my kids to stir and counter, "We won't know until we try it." When we picked Alex and Ryan up, my grandmother would laugh and say, "I tried." My mom would give us a bag of cookies with Doritos and cereal in them, along with our very excited children, telling us, "You will eat them, and you will like them."

My grandmother, Grandma Butch, was a 5'2" tour de force who raised seven children in a two-bedroom, two-bathroom Cape Cod in Ferguson, MO. My grandfather gave her that nickname because he felt it was so far from her demeanor and stature. I adored her. My grandma Butch had a wicked sense of humor, was sneaky good at cards and appreciated a perfect Manhattan. She was a devout Catholic. For her, there was engagement, then marriage, then moving in. Rob had to be introduced to the family at a holiday gathering before any of this. For any of us with a serious relationship, this was a big deal. My grandma absolutely adored Rob. Just before he and I moved in together before we got married, I had dinner with her. She looked at me sternly in her tiny kitchen. She said, "I don't approve of any of this. Now come with me so I can get you some pots so you can cook that boy some decent food." It's one of my enduring memories of her.

In July 2008, my father was diagnosed with stage 4 lung cancer. He only lived a few months, passing away a few days before Christmas. The following year, my grandmother passed away in her sleep during Memorial Day weekend. My mom was her caregiver, and the stress of that caused my mom to have several small strokes and fall into dementia. She never said my name or my kids' names again. She died a few days before the following Christmas. Within the span of a year, I had lost three of the most important people in the world to me. I felt a little untethered, a little less rooted in the world. Every time something incredible happened, I instinctively picked up the phone to call them. Every time something challenging happened, I instinctively picked up the phone to call for advice. Suddenly I was on my own.

And I needed them. My health began to fail. The career that I loved was suddenly falling away. My husband lost his job. Both of my kids got seriously injured playing sports, and my son received his Autism diagnosis. That was when my girlfriends truly became my sisters. Over margaritas with cute shoes and sparkly tops, they gave me shoulders to cry on, tough love, and an ever-needed perspective. I would get through this. And most of all, I wasn't alone.

I poured myself into work. When I started working in preschools 30 years before, I was in high school. When people asked who I was, I said I was a mom, a wife, and a teacher. It was all I knew. I had worked with families and kids from across the globe of all ages. I had worked with kids from wealth and kids who only got meals at our schools. I remember vividly the child who was being fostered by his grandmother. She was late to pick him up. When she did, she was angry and agitated. I followed her out to her car and asked her if I could help her. She punched him 3 times before unlocking his seatbelt, pushing him out of the still parked car, and driving away. I picked up that little boy and called the child abuse hotline. I held him until the police arrived to take him to a children's shelter. I visited him a week or so later. He laid on the floor and clung to my feet when

I left, begging me to stay. I never saw him again, but his face remains burned in my memory. As do the faces of so many children that I've taught. The five-year-old Autistic boy who sang his first words, Old McDonald, while cuddled up in my lap. The baby would greet me by scooting on his bottom across the entire classroom to point out his favorite toys. The little girl from Russia that I walked miles through the halls with only two words was Krolik (bunny) and Privyet (hello).

I loved the kids. I loved the parents. I loved nothing more than being in the classrooms and seeing those moments of pure joy when kids would suddenly figure out a little more about how their world worked. You and I would get bored blowing dandelion fluff once. A two-year-old? They'd do that for an hour if you let them.

Now, after almost 30 years, those squeals of delight that I loved so much were starting to cause searing pain in my head. The sunlight on the playground was beginning to make me nauseous. I began to retreat into my darkened office, away from my classrooms, away from my kids. I hated it. My body was breaking down. I was exhausted, and I was sick. And I needed help.

They started when I was ten. I can remember that first night like it was yesterday. I woke up screaming, rolled into a ball, with my hands over my ears. My eyes were squeezed tight against invading light. The pain in my head was overwhelming. I was dizzy, and I felt like I was going to throw up. Despite my eyes being closed, lights were popping in my eyes like fireworks, threatening to make me vomit. The intermittent cars driving past my front-facing window felt like they were roaring next to me at full volume. All of it threatened to overwhelm me, to take me under, to drown me in a sea of pain.

My mom and dad were at my side in moments. Bone-chilling screams from your ten-year-old daughter have a way of motivating you to action. My dad instinctively turned on the lights, and I howled. The lights were quickly extinguished. My mom got some medicine and a cool washcloth for my neck. She rubbed my neck until I fell into a fitful sleep. I didn't go to school for two days.

That was my first migraine. But not my last. At ten, it was chalked up to stress. Well-meaning people whispered to my parents, "Poor thing, what does she have to be so stressed about at that age?" I saw my first doctor at 11 and was put on the first of a revolving series of medications that I would have with me for the rest of my life. Pediatricians evolved into neurologists. In college, I started losing sight in one eye during attacks. In my 20's and 30's, my hands and face started going numb, and I had trouble speaking when I had migraines. Attacks that once lasted a couple of hours now lasted days. Before long, I started to look like I was having a stroke—the right side of my face would lose feeling and begin to droop. I had vertigo, tremors, and trouble with motor control. I would become so disoriented that I got lost in my neighborhood. By the time I was hiding in my dark office, I had symptoms 25 days a month, and I was in the hospital monthly.

At some point, the words describing my condition changed from "migraine" to Complex Reticular Hemiplegic Migraine with Vestibular Disturbance. Doctors with lots of letters behind their names put complicated words to what was happening to my body, what would continue to happen to my body, and what was likely to happen to my children. My specific type of migraine is genetic, involves multiple symptoms, typically affects one side of my body, and has no known triggers. It's progressive, so there are likely more symptoms coming. Attacks come without warning. They may be nothing more than exhaustion for 30 minutes or maybe more than a week of crippling pain, loss of control of part of my body and speech, and disorientation.

Living with a neurodegenerative disease is not easy. It's a separate full-time job. Doctors. A revolving door of medications. Diets. New therapies. Expensive scans won't tell you anything new, but you need to make sure that the new symptoms are well, just new symptoms, and not something more insidious. Slowly but surely, your world becomes smaller and smaller. What aggravates your illness is weeded out, and the things that keep the illness at bay are kept. Doctors remind you of the importance of being compliant. And you are for a while. Until you're not. Until you simply can't take it anymore. Until you can't take not being normal. Until you need that margarita night with the girls and having a Diet Coke reminds you of just how "other" you are. At that moment, having that sense of normalcy keeps your world a little bigger, even if it's just for one night.

I don't think it's a coincidence that my One New Thing Project started ramping up as illness started going bananas. When I started the project, I was doing one, maybe two things a month if I was feeling ambitious. As my attacks began getting worse and more frequent, I started doing more new things without even realizing it. It was a way to push the limits on my artificially contracted world. To bring back some semblance of control. To bring back some semblance of joy.

Complex Reticular Hemiplegic Migraine is genetic. Both of my kids were probably going to develop it as well. My daughter, Alex, started having a few in middle school, but they hit hard in high school and then cranked up the volume in college. Now, as an adult, her symptoms are similar to mine. For Ryan, his headaches made their appearance in high school after an injury. His are at a low level, but every single day. Relentless. For me, being in a busy, noisy building full of 160 exuberant kids under 5 did nothing but intensify with an illness that gets worse with lots of noise and light. At the time, I couldn't bear the thought of giving up 30 years in that life--of shrinking my world so much—of losing such a very fundamental part of me. I was still young. What would I even do?

The decision of whether or not to leave my job was much bigger than an identity crisis. Just before I started the One New Thing Project, Rob was laid off from what appeared to be a stable job at a Fortune 500 company. He had been there for 17 years. There wasn't much severance. We tried not to keep things from our kids. With something so major, Rob and I had agreed that if he didn't find a job within a couple of months, all of us would need to make a sacrifice. That meant the activities that gave Alex and Ryan stability and many of their friends. They needed to know as soon as possible. They were incredibly perceptive and always had a way of sniffing things out. I made cookies on the day that my mom died, and to this day, they ask me who died when I randomly make chocolate chip cookies. It's been 11 years, and my kids are now adults.

We had no clue how to tell our children that their father had been laid off, and there was a big possibility that they wouldn't be able to keep doing the things they loved with their friends. So we took them to our local Chinese buffet. We thought that should buy us some time to figure out how to start this conversation while they stuff their mouths with crab Rangoon and ice cream. Rob and I kept shooting glances at each other over our free refills, silently asking each other, "Are you going to start this off?" "Umm…no… I'm positive we agreed that YOU were going to start this."

The bill finally came with four fortune cookies. It was now or never. Alex and Ryan opened theirs. I opened mine. Then Rob opened his and threw back his head in laughter. He handed it to me. "You will experience a change of job." I started laughing. Conversation started. Thanks, fortune cookie. Alex pulled the fortune from my hand. She and Ryan read it and stared at that beady "mom's making cookies, who died" stare. Rob rubbed his eyes and said, "Well, that's one way to tell you that dad got laid off."

Rob was out of work for 3 months. Less than we expected, but enough to do some damage. We pinched every penny we could and were able to keep the kids in their activities. Alex was playing field hockey for a prominent club that was touring the United States. At 14, she was part of the Olympic Development program, with her sights set on the Rio Olympics. She ran cross country and picked up track in the off-season. She had a promising future as a pole vaulter. Then during a warm-up when she was 16, she tore her ACL. She played field hockey and vaulted on that knee for an entire season before it was diagnosed. By then, the damage was done. Even with surgery and a year of rehab with an airplane-grade titanium brace on her leg, it would never be the same. She would always dismiss any pain that she felt when she played or ran, afraid that the doctors would pull the plug. Her senior season, she ran and vaulted with a compression fracture in her shin, collapsing at the finish line of her last race after beating her personal best. She would never play field hockey, run competitively, or vault again.

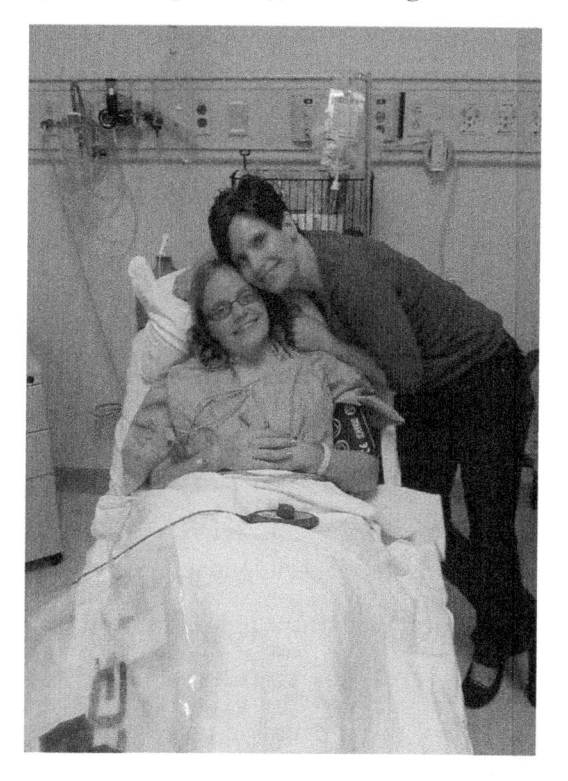

A year after Alex tore her ACL and thought she was into recovery, Ryan got hurt playing hockey. Ryan was always small for his age. He didn't hit 100 pounds until he was 15. That was a condition for him to get his driver's permit. But what he lacked in size, he made up for in attitude. In high school hockey, he was the one who stood up to other players for any infractions, real or perceived. In the mind of a high school hockey player, there are plenty of perceived infractions. In one game, an opposing player clearly had had enough of Ryan's mouth, and given the fact that Ryan came up to his mid-chest, he was an easy target. The other player checked him at a faceoff, and Ryan fell back, hitting his head on the ice. Ryan stayed on the ice, cradling his head. I silently prayed that Ryan was playing it up to get a penalty called for the other player. It worked. But Ryan wasn't playing it up.

The next day Ryan had a headache, the first he'd ever had. That headache would continue the next day for every day after that. Ryan had a concussion, and while most people recover fairly quickly from concussions, Ryan wasn't most people. Concussions make any issue you have worse. Ryan was genetically predisposed to migraines, so the headaches weren't going to go away without a fight. His Autism also makes him prone to his eyes not working together, something called nystagmus. So, the concussion made that worse. We spent 3 years driving across the state, taking him to specialists in Kansas City as well as a variety of other specialists. We finally just started calling the doctors by the numbers. Doctor 4 confirmed Ryan's Autism diagnosis, something Ryan's talented early childhood teacher mentioned when he was 18 months old. Doctor 11 shared Ryan's love for the movie the Departed. Doctor 12 got a dozen donuts. When the physical therapist assigned us to take Ryan to a playground to have him swing until he got dizzy, Alex was excited to help. His eyes didn't work together. He got dizzy very quickly, and after 60 seconds or so, Ryan would get off the swings, take a couple of steps, and fall over like he had drunk a fifth of Jack Daniels. As a mom, I felt truly awful watching it (now, there's a lot of humor in the memory). If Alex could have YouTube'd that at the time, she would have won the internet.

Going through all of that in a very short period of time was hard. Hard on all of us. All I can say is thank whoever you pray to that it did not happen all at once. But here's the thing. We all survived. And we got some pretty good stories coming at the end of it. Alex, to this day, teases Ryan about those days on the playground. Even my mom's funeral has great stories around it, and my mom would have loved that.

I was finding the beginnings of joy, even in those difficult and turbulent times. Joy isn't something that comes easy. It's a lot like a stool with four legs, and without any one of those, you're tipping over. You have to be able to hold on to the good things while simultaneously being able to move past the tough parts, keep your mind from wandering, and be able to give and receive freely. This was the magic of doing new things during that time. As I had one hard thing that was tough to get through, I also had a new thing, often a small thing like trying new food, to help me hold on to the good and truly savor the moment in front of me. That also allowed me to be grateful for the love and generosity that continues to be shared with me.

THE RULES OF THE GAME

Making the Most of Your One New Thing Project

I'M STANDING AT MY KITCHEN COUNTER in a pink pineapple apron. Across the granite from me is a cell phone on a tripod manned by my husband, Rob. I've studied the recipe in front of me five times. I've got milk in a pot on the stove. The counter in front of me has a cutting board with a couple of spatulas, measured out kosher salt, rennet tablets, and citric acid. I look like Julia Childs. Julia maybe didn't have the glass of wine, but I've got some nerves. Although the recipe says this is supposed to be undeniably easy, something even a mediocre cook like myself can do, my first Facebook Live is doing a new thing. In a few moments, unsuspecting viewers will watch me either make mozzarella from scratch in 30 minutes or make a disaster in my kitchen. I gulp down the wine. Truth be told, I'm betting on the latter.

    The video rolls on, and I meticulously follow the recipe. As I wait for the curds and whey to separate, there's just unending dead air. I take another swig of wine. I try to banter with Rob. He grins back and gives me a thumbs up. Thanks, bro.

    It's been 30 minutes, and I have no mozzarella. More wine. More dead air. I'm filling it with meaningless chatter. Julia never had this problem. 45 minutes. No cheese. An hour and 15 minutes, and I'm genuinely apologizing to the people who are watching for wasting their time.

    Finally, I have some formed blobs that I can do something with. The next step is to dump them into the salty liquid whey and then stretch the blobs into real mozzarella. I'm a little behind, but I can still salvage this. I dump a blob into the whey, and it immediately disintegrates into a zillion floating boogers. I'm at a loss for words. I look at the bowl of liquid and floating goo. Nothing to be salvaged there. I'm like a kid whose puppy just ran away.

That was New Thing number 265--making mozzarella from scratch, and that's the way new things go sometimes. Even when you think you know what you're doing--even when you think you've read all of the instructions and are completely prepared, sometimes things just go sideways. I was extremely disappointed with that one because number 264 that same day was doing my first Facebook Live. Even though doing over 260 new things gave me a fresh outlook on dealing with failure, perfectionism was poking me in the back the entire time. As my recipe was falling apart, and as silence hung around me, I just kept thinking to myself, *"Who do you think you are? You know you're no Julia Childs."*

Making mozzarella was never necessarily on my bucket list, but I like cheese, and I like to eat. As you'll find out, I'm a pretty terrible cook, but trying new recipes was a way for me to begin to dip my toes into doing new things. The One New Thing Project, which for me began almost a decade ago, started as a list of things to do and rapidly became much more than that. It became about shifting how you interact with your world and the people around you to actively seek out and find things that bring you joy. When you do that on a routine basis, you're in the driver's seat, and you begin to intentionally choose what you allow into your life. You slowly start to distance yourself from the things that don't or that actively bring you discomfort. That gives you a certain amount of power, even in circumstances where you feel like you have no control. You begin to identify small elements that do make you joyful--things like the sun shining through the clouds or a good cup of coffee. Something that you may have overlooked before.

Over the last nine and a half years, I've been at various stages with my One New Thing Project. I've been inundated with new things to do. I've been at a complete loss for them, with the end of the month drawing near and scratching for something to do. I've done terrifying things, and I've done exhilarating things. I was building this from the ground up, and that in itself was a new thing. I've learned a few things along the way that I hope will make your experience a richer one.

The One New Thing Project is an intensely personal one with far-reaching ripples. The more joy that we're able to find, the more joy we can share with others. As we're able to intentionally choose our relationships and our environments, we can bring our whole selves into those situations more of the time. That means we're giving the very best of ourselves all the time. Our relationships get better and deeper. We communicate better because we're paying more attention. Our kids get all of us when we're with them because we're not too worn out from giving too much of ourselves in other places. Our work feels more fulfilling because we can find the places where we make the most impact--the places that push our happy buttons. My marriage with Rob became much deeper and stronger. We found many more common interests. We talk more about more important things now than we ever did, and we certainly laugh more. You have to when you blow up chocolate bowls all over your kitchen ceiling or when you're figuring out how to paddleboard. Trust, communication, and humor give you the strength to get through really hard things. It's not easy to be married to someone with a neurodegenerative disease or mental illness. Rob gets to live with both of those. You have to be able to talk about everything to make it through that. This project taught us that we can.

Rule #1-Keep Your Focus on Joy

Your One New Thing Project is all about what brings you joy. As you'll learn, it's very different from a bucket list, and it's not intended to be a list that you check things off of. You'll find things that you will want to keep in your life forever, and some things that you'll do once, and that will be enough. For starters, look at what you know that brings you joy already and see if you can take one step outside of that box. Do you like to try new restaurants? Maybe give a new cuisine a try. Do you like to work out? How about mixing it up with a different kind of exercise?

Rule #2-Be Consistent

As I watch people start their own One New Thing Projects, being consistent is probably the most significant predictor of whether or not they will be successful. Doing new things regularly not only helps us get more comfortable with ever-widening the box we unwittingly live in. It retrains our brain to pick out novel things in the world that we are already doing. Regular looks like a lot of things to a lot of people. It may be once a week, once a month, or once a quarter. My suggestion is to start with once a month and go from there. Once a month is frequent enough to keep it fresh in mind that you're not going to forget about it. Still, it's not so often that you feel like it's an assignment, and you find yourself stressing out about figuring out which new thing you're going to do next. That's especially helpful at the beginning. I found that once I got in the groove of doing new things, I looked for them more often than once a month. Better still, they sort of fell into my lap. As time went on, I ended up averaging about three new things a month. Your results may vary. I know that it's easier to start slow and then up your game later, so if you feel comfortable with it once a quarter, go for it. If once a month is more your speed, terrific. Just make sure that you're doing new things on a regular basis.

Rule #3-Set a Timeline

It's important to give yourself time to get into the groove of doing new things. By definition, doing new things is itself a new thing for you. You'll need a little time for your body and mind to adjust to that. If you're planning to try something new once a month, give yourself six months at least to start. If you want to try something every three or four months, give it a year. As time goes on and you start doing new things consistently, your brain will notice opportunities for even more unique experiences that you hadn't seen before. And that's when the magic starts to happen. Think about a timeline that makes the most sense for your life and make a plan for it. If you worry about fitting new things in, go with a longer timeline (say, quarterly) and build up more often. You can always add more experiences in between as they pop up.

Rule #4-Write Down Your Experiences

If I could only give you one piece of advice when you start your One New Thing Project, this would be it. Document your new things. You will do many exciting things—personal things, fun things, and yes, things that are failures. You will learn from all of them. You will want to look back at all of them. Trust me when I say you will not remember them all. Take pictures, write notes. Do whatever documentation makes sense for you to capture the memory. Weeks, months, and years later, when the experience has faded a bit, you will want something to look back at to remind you of your adventures. My first new things were posted on Facebook, so nearly every day now, I get a memory of something interesting I've done. It's a great way to start your day.

Documenting your experiences also helps you stick to your timeline for doing new things—especially if you're starting out. This is even more important if your new things are spaced out a couple of months. You're going to need help keeping track of when you did what. Plus, there's just something about writing your experiences down and sharing them with others. People begin to ask you about what you're doing—what new things you've done, how you liked them, and what you're doing next. They offer suggestions about what you can do next and start to cheer you on. You even find people to join you on different experiences. It becomes a community effort, and that helps you be a whole lot more successful.

Documenting what you do also gives you a way to reflect on the things you're doing. Did you like your experience? Is it something you'd do again? Was there anything that stood out to you? I have found that reflection has been an invaluable part of this process. Every Facebook or blog post that I have done has included what the new thing was and often included a picture and something special about that experience. Going back months, or sometimes years later, I started to see how one new thing led me to another and how each thing affected me. I could only see the full story of my One New Thing Project because I had documented what I had done pretty well.

I say that I had documented my One New Thing Project pretty well because I've tried a few different things over the last several years. That's left me with some new things that fell through the cracks (every now and again, Facebook reminds me of one I've forgotten) and some definite opinions about what works well and what doesn't. It's also worth noting that how you keep track of your new things is a personal choice, so take my recommendations and apply them to you.

When I started the One New Thing Project, I promised to post my new things on Facebook. That was my way of holding myself accountable to the world, and at the time, it seemed like a pretty good way of keeping track of everything. I also didn't plan on doing the project for almost a decade. After a while, I moved to a blog on Tumblr and then went legit and started writing on theonenewthingproject.com. I still share a lot of my experiences on Facebook, Instagram, and Twitter, but they are no longer my primary source for documenting and storing my memories, and they shouldn't be for you, either.

There are a few reasons that social media is a bad idea for primary documenting. It is awful for searching. I mean, truly awful. I always used the hashtag #myonenewthing on my experiences, which didn't even help me find what I was looking for. Even after spending hours poring over my memories, photos, and posts, and those of my family to find every last new thing, we missed a couple dozen. They keep popping up on memories, and I add them to the archive that I have now.

The other reason that you should be wary of using social media for your primary storage is that community standards are forever changing. Since the beginning of my project, everything that I've done has had to be "Facebook appropriate" since I had agreed to post the details on Facebook. However, when I went back to catalog all of my memories, I came across one with a blocked picture with a warning that it didn't meet community standards. When I clicked the warning, I recognized the original post from when I got my first hot stone massage. It was a picture of a massage bed with a Pepto Bismol pink blanket covering it. The post read, "My first hot stone massage. This is as far as you go." Just remember that algorithms don't have a sense of humor. If you're using social media for your primary storage, you're likely to lose some memories at some point.

After that experience with social media, I learned to save my memories in triplicate. I save all of my photos to a Dropbox folder with subfolders for each year. However, not all of my experiences are photo-worthy or appropriate. Sometimes, you just don't have your phone handy, and I've learned that sometimes it's better just to be in the experience fully and not worry about trying to snap a cute selfie. I'll write down the story later. For that, I love the Speechy app. Speechy takes dictation and texts or emails you so you can just gush about how cool your new thing was. No muss, no fuss. Then you can copy and paste that into whatever you're using to keep track of your experiences.

If you're a journal person, you may want to get a cool notebook to keep pictures, mementos, and notes about everything you're doing. If you're looking for a place to get started, check out www.theonenewthingproject.com for a cool e-journal that lets you record your photos, memories and has a few ideas to get you started. Don't be afraid to get creative with how you keep track of things, though. There's a little German settlement not far from our house that's known for wineries. Rob and I spent our anniversary there this year (another new thing). At a local whiskey distillery, we picked up a leather box with maps printed on it. This year, we're going to make a time capsule of our new things with that box.

Because I frequently go back to the new things that I've done in the past, I created a searchable spreadsheet of everything that I've done. It has photos, plus a couple of notes about each experience. You can find the spreadsheet template at www.theonenewthingproject.com. That helped me get ideas for new things, blogging, and keeping track of what I've already done. I'm also creating a photo book for each year. I include pictures, some of my memories, and some quotes that fit the experiences. I'm a pretty tangible person, so I like to have things to hold in my hands, to thumb through and look at. I like the idea of having all of my new things in a collection to hold in my hands, and I like the idea of being able to hand that to my grandkids when I'm old. Proof that grandma was pretty cool back in the day.

Rule #5-Try Everything Twice

Ok, this will come up in detail later, and I don't want to spoil the story. For now, I'm just going to say that you need to trust me on this. We're all different. Just because a new thing didn't go the way you planned for it to go doesn't mean it was a complete failure. It just means it didn't go the way *you planned it*. My motto has become to *"Try everything twice."* Try it first for the experience. Try it the second time to make sure you did it the way it was intended for you. At least you'll get a good story from it. In my experience, the second time usually goes a heck of a lot better when you consider your personal attributes.

How Do You Decide on Your New Things?

Just as your new thing project is a very personal thing, so are the new things you're going to do. I've done everything from eating mooncakes to visiting Mexico to running half-marathons to experiencing my first Mardi Gras. Only had one of those things was on my original list of new things that I wanted to try. On the other hand, I'm super claustrophobic. I hate caves. If you asked me when this started if I'd ever go caving, the answer would have been a resounding no. However, I have played paintball in a giant cavern big enough to drive trucks through, and that wasn't so scary. We went snorkeling in the cenotes during a trip to Mexico. Cenotes are open cave chambers with natural groundwater. Our guide was accustomed to cave diving and exploring from the cenotes to the ocean in that excursion. Without warning, he took us into some tight spots. While it was scary for me, I survived that, and after taking a few deep breaths, I enjoyed it. Now, one of my best friends has tons of experience exploring caves. So would I go caving now? With him, probably. It's all about baby steps, you all.

    The world around you is full of new things to explore. You don't need to take a big vacation to do them, you don't need to face huge fears, and you don't need to have some life-changing moment, although I will tell you that one or more of those are side effects of the One New Thing Project. To figure out what your new things could be, start with a list. What have you always wanted to try? What did 13 years old you want to do that you never got around to? What intrigues you but scares you just a hair? Ask your friends what they've always wanted to try. Think back to those conversations that ended with "we should do that...." That's a good place to start.

You'll find ideas in this book and ideas about how to think about finding ideas. You're going to find a lot of new ways of thinking about a lot of things. This book is all about finding your inner three-year-old's joy that's been hidden away, pushed down. Let them come out to play.

In the end, your One New Thing Project is yours alone. As you'll see, new things are not always about big, giant, scary things. Many of my most memorable new things were spontaneous, in-the-moment sparks of amazingness or tiny blips that you might miss if you weren't looking for them. They are the things that I treasure—the moments that I hold when I'm having a rough time. They remind me that I can do hard things. They remind me of the huge amount of joy in my life, and without a doubt, they have provided my family and me with the very best stories we have.

The Rules of The Game

BIG THINGS AND SMALL THINGS

Sushi, Broken Eggs, and Dancing

DID YOU KNOW THAT YOU CAN swim with wild pigs? Yes. That is a real thing in the Bahamas. Well, a part of the Bahamas is called the Exumas. I have many questions about this. Like why do pigs swim in the ocean? Why would you want to swim with them? I'm fairly grossed out by seaweed. What happens to the pig poop?

Here's my point. When you start doing new things, you may be ready to hop a plane to the Exumas and dive in with wild pigs. I was not. I needed to get my feet wet trying new things first (see what I did there?).

That's why just a few months after I started the project, I found myself sitting across from my teenage kids at the tiny sushi restaurant around the corner from my house, about as far as you can get in principle from swimming with wild pigs. One is eyeing the plate of rice, seaweed, and raw fish in between us with a dose of skepticism. The other is nearly dancing out of her chair with glee. We've passed this tiny family restaurant a hundred times, and today was the day we were trying sushi for the first time. Alex is getting impatient. She starts to goad her brother. "Geez, Ryan, just try it!" She's delighting at this moment because there is a very strong possibility that Ryan will make some sort of overly dramatic reaction, up to and including spitting the entire thing out on his plate. We've seen this before with basically any food that's not breaded or tacos.

Ryan continues to look skeptically at the sushi. I reach down with my chopsticks, and after several failed attempts, I manage to grab a California roll. With my mouth full, I give it a thumbs up. "Ryaaaaaaan...." His sister sighs loudly. She's pushing the right buttons now. I know this play. I know where it's going. Wait for it...

"FINE. " Ryan brings down his chopsticks and lifts an innocuous-looking piece of sushi into his mouth. He pulls a face briefly, then gives a hand sign for "so-so" with his mouth stuffed. For Ryan, this constitutes five stars. Alex grins in victory. Ryan isn't usually known for trying the new, the different, and the weird. Alex has always been his Sherpa with that, and like all good siblings, they kept a lot of those adventures hidden from mom and dad until they safely reached adulthood.

That was our first experience with sushi, but it was far from our last. I fell in love with it, and funny enough, so did Ryan. Alex, not so much. Eating sushi was a big new thing for us. We ate pretty much the same thing for dinner every single night. Alex still teases that she can tell you what we ate based on what day of the week it was. There were a lot of reasons for that. We led a super busy life, and some meals work way better on nights with practice and Girl Scouts. I am objectively a terrible cook and can only make about six edible meals. An Autistic kid works way better with a predictable routine. But mostly, we were broke. Y'all, I was a preschool director, and my husband was a

Big Things and Small Things

communications specialist. Those jobs don't make a lot of money. We bought a bunch of stuff at Costco and just made the same stuff over and over.

So, if we didn't have a lot of disposable income, and we didn't have the mindset for big crazy new things, swimming with wild pigs in the Exumas certainly wasn't on our radar—pig poop in the ocean or not. But sushi was something we could handle.

When people ask me about the One New Thing Project, they often assume it's a bucket list. I get how they can be confused but let me just clear that up now. The One New Thing Project and your bucket list may have some overlapping things, but the ideas behind them are pretty different. I may be going out on a limb here, but if you asked 100 people if sushi were on their bucket list, you're probably not going to get a whole lot of takers. Your bucket list is all the stuff that you want to do when your time is limited—those big, once in a life, moon-shot kinds of things. Most people of a certain age (ahem...) have a bucket list. We know what's on it, thinking longingly of the days we can ditch the responsibilities to go and summit Mt. Everest. Your one new thing list is not that. It includes things you've always wanted to try, things you're terrified of, things you're curious about, foods you want to eat, places you want to visit, big things, small things, free things, and expensive things. By its very nature, it's incomplete and ever-expanding. While you start with an idea of what you want to do, unlike your bucket list, you don't necessarily know what will be on your new thing list until those things show up in front of you and you decide to try them.

There are a few misnomers that need some clarifying when it comes to trying new things. The first is that all New Things have to be big scary things. They don't. I'm not a thrill-seeker for reasons I'll explain shortly. I may skydive someday. My daughter sure thinks I will. But the One New Thing Project is about finding ways to open yourself to new experiences in your daily life--frequently. Some of those experiences will be one-time-only things, like when I saw the Christmas star—when Jupiter and Saturn align to create a brilliant light in the southwest sky just before Christmas. It only happens every 800 years. Some of those experiences will be things you'll decide to do every now and again. We fell in love with kayaking and decided to do that periodically. Some will become a part of your life for a long time. I started running to do a 5k and ran for several years, completing several half marathons. Believe me, I never thought I wanted to do that when I started. I thought people that ran were absolutely insane.

As humans are hardwired to avoid many new experiences, we must make an intentional effort to do it. Our predecessors couldn't exactly try a lot of new plants and survive, could they? I think about that every time I see a jackfruit. Who was the first person to decide it was a good idea to eat *that thing*?

We start with one thing. We do that one thing until we get comfortable, and then we try another. And then another. And slowly, our little world starts to get a tiny bit bigger. We started with sushi, and now anytime we find a new kind of cuisine, we chat with the restaurant owners to help us find the best food and help us learn how to eat it to get the most out of it. That's how we learned about Ethiopia and its food at a little restaurant in our city center. The proprietor patiently piled on different kinds of wat with injera (flatbread). She taught us how to pinch pieces of the injera and pick up the wat with our hands. Then she told us about her home and how she came to our city. Before sushi, that never would have been possible. There are lots of good reasons to start small. It's a good way to test your comfort level with change and risk. And let me tell you, both of those are important in what we're doing.

What we each find interesting and compelling is an individual thing. One of the things that come with Ryan's Autism is Sensory Integration Disorder. His body has difficulty integrating the sensations that he takes in from the outside world. Everything from tags on clothes to spices on food presents massive challenges to him--hence our highly structured menu. Ryan hates roller coasters. They make him incredibly ill. That's why, after his concussion, he couldn't swing on playground swings for more than 60 seconds without looking completely drunk. Alex still gives him trouble for all of the roller coasters she feels jilted out of in her youth over this. I have a friend who organizes his vacations to visit every single twisty, loopy, high-speed roller coaster in the country. The moral of the story? Not all of us are fit for roller coasters, and not all of us are fit for flat land. Different strokes, my friends.

Each of us has a different threshold for the amount of new stuff we want to take in. Each of us is uniquely different in how we approach new experiences and sensations. We all fall at a different place along a scale, depending on the types of experiences we want to have and how intense we want our experiences to be--everyone from the thrill seeker to the homebody. Your traits are your starting point in the race—how far forward or far back you are. You can stay there, or you can move, depending on what you do in your life. For example, suppose you are born a feet-on-the-ground homebody and never expose yourself to new experiences. In that case, you'll always stay exactly there. However, if you try a few new things here and there, now your feet-on-the-ground homebody-self moves up the scale a notch or two.

Your roller coaster, dance on the bar types? You're probably already trying a few new things. Why? Because it's easier for you. Your body and mind crave that stimulation. So, for you, eating sushi probably looks kind of lame. You may be looking at doing bigger, bolder things. That will move you down the scale faster. Which is great. Until it's not. People at the top end of the scale often underestimate the risk of their actions. And that's where it's helpful to try smaller new things—to be a bit more mindful. If folks at the lower end take small steps to learn to trust taking risks, it's helpful for folks at the top end of the scale to take small steps to reel you back in before you leap, so to speak.

Trying new things can be a complicated endeavor. For me, when it came right down to it, it was a matter of trust. Did I trust myself to do this thing? Would it be safe? Would I be good at it? To be honest, it's easier to make that jump when you're talking about sushi or reading that book you were supposed to in high school but can finally appreciate now, or going to that historic donut shop that is an hour away. But to paraphrase Neil Armstrong, one small step for you, one big step for your life.

Aside from the fact that small things are generally cheap or free and pretty easy to do, there was one big reason I started off doing a lot of small things. I didn't trust myself with big things.

I grew up in a working-class Catholic family on the Southside of St. Louis. My mom was a nurse, my dad was an accountant. As a kid, I thought I had a pretty typical family. My parents sacrificed a lot to make sure that my brother and I went to Catholic school through high school. All girls for me, all boys for him. They gave us a lot of opportunities. But I was largely unaware of the struggles that my parents faced. My mom struggled with serious depression. My dad, a Vietnam vet, drank heavily to stave off PTSD. They didn't talk much, and a month before I graduated from high school, it all fell apart. My parents separated a month before their 20th wedding anniversary.

Ending their marriage was costly. My dad got a small one-bedroom apartment, and a couple of weeks later, my mom got a job offer to start a new AIDS clinic an hour and a half away. Going from one household to two meant smaller homes, and mom got a one bedroom as well. My brother would crash on the couch when he came home from college, but I would need to stay behind while we worked out the sale of our family home. College for me for that year was put to the side. A couple of weeks before I graduated high school at 17, I was desperately hunting for roommates, a full-time job that would help me cover the mortgage and utilities of the house.

What transpired over the next year was an exercise in survival. I got a minimum wage job as a teacher's aide in a childcare center. A girl that I graduated with knew someone she worked with at a restaurant looking for a place to live. On our meager salaries (my $4.25 an hour and their $2.12 an hour plus tips), we managed to cobble together a little family. Dinner consisted of knock-off ramen and mac and cheese most nights.

We managed to keep the mortgage paid and fix the boiler when it broke, although that meant that at times, we were without one or more of our utilities. We had a note on our refrigerator with a prioritized list of our utilities:

1. Gas (to heat water for baths and cook with)
2. Electricity (we could go by candlelight and cook canned and boxed food if needed)
3. Water (we would frequently steal water from our neighbor's hose faucet by the potful to keep our 1 toilet running, bath, and cook with).

I managed to take a few classes at the local community college as well. A year later, after we freshened up the house with some borrowed paint, it was sold. Although we had plenty of notice, I was left without a place to go. My roommates were moving on to live with their boyfriend and girlfriend, respectfully, so I was on my own. Unable to afford an apartment, I was officially homeless. Thankfully, a friend stepped in to help. He arranged an interview for admission into his college for the summer term that had just begun. That led to me moving into campus on an emergency basis to take classes through work-study. I moved my meager belongings into a small dorm room and felt like I could breathe for the first time in a year. And life went on.

I tell people that story now, as an adult, and they stare at me slack-jawed. It never occurred to me that it was a strange way to move into adulthood. It was just what happened. What that year taught me was that there was little room for error. I was already a twitchy little perfectionist. I credit my fifth-grade teacher, Sr. Damien, a stern woman with square glasses and a ruler who enjoyed telling children they were too stupid to amount to much, for starting me on that road. There's a whole generation of students from Holy Family in St. Louis that twitch when they see nuns because of her.

During the year after high school, everything hinged around keeping the right balance of money, time, and resources. Giving up stale ramen for McDonald's meant that the gas bill may not be paid, and everyone in the house was taking cold baths because of you. At a certain point, you stop indulging. You stop taking risks, no matter how small--you stop trusting yourself to take them.

Most people that I share this story with tell me that is NOT how most families function. And that's a good thing. But if you look deep, in your heart of hearts, there are probably some things that you have a hard time trusting yourself with as well. We tend to be overly hard on ourselves, much harder than we are on others. We feel like we have to earn small indulgences. We don't deserve to reward ourselves under any circumstances. I'm often stunned by how we talk to ourselves. Small new things are your opportunity to give yourself a break. To have your cake and eat it too. To indulge in a little bit of joy, with no guilt and no shame. To take time and space for you and enjoy it, the risk is relatively low, but the reward potential is pretty high.

I also find that I seek out small new things when I'm feeling overwhelmed. Small things have a particular kind of mindfulness to them that brings me immense satisfaction. One of my favorite small things that I ever did was learning to play a Tibetan singing bowl. Singing bowls are metal or crystal bowls played by drawing a wooden mallet around the outside edge. It takes practice, and it takes a little precision, but once you get the knack of it, these little bowls suddenly have this sound that comes from nowhere. And it's so loud! And soothing. Oh my gosh! You can feel the frequency reverberating through your hand in a way that brings your total focus to just that point. Everything else melts away. It's a magical experience. Have I convinced you? Take a look on YouTube, or better yet, visit a sound bath at a local yoga studio if you want to try it before you buy. A sound bath is an incredible experience. Your entire job is to relax. The instructor plays a series of singing bowls at different frequencies and other instruments to complement the singing bowls. The singing bowls are chosen to slowly start you meditating and into deeper and deeper relaxation. You finish the sound bath feeling completely refreshed.

In 2018, we visited the Festival of Nations for the first time. This annual festival in the 289-acre park across the street from the home where I grew up showcased the cultures from hundreds of nations that called our city home. The festival is a magical place of food, crafts, and dance. They even have food from our favorite Ethiopian restaurant. And there, in one of the booths, was a man from Tibet with singing bowls. He showed me how to play and encouraged me to try several different bowls to find one I liked. I took one home and sat with this little brass bowl in my hands, circling the mallet around the rim until its tone warmed from the center. When I stopped, the sound hung in the air for several seconds, then slowly floated away. Taking with it all of my worries and leaving me completely at peace.

You don't need a Tibetan singing bowl or sound bath when you're stressed. But small things can be a shortcut to getting out of that survival, everything is stressful mode. And really, any small new thing will do. When we're under stress, our primitive "fight or flight, protect me" brain takes over. All of a sudden, that person we work with doesn't seem very helpful. She seems like a conniving you-know-what, hell-bent on making us look bad. Our brain is faking threats everywhere. Since we're focused on surviving, risks start looking a whole lot more like threats, and we're risking life and limb if we go out looking for big risks. That primitive part of the brain starts to take logical thinking and language out of the equation (I mean, that person at work is just offering you coffee, but logical thinking is out the window here). Your brain starts to go on autopilot, assessing threats and keeping you safe. The interesting thing is that like autopilot on a plane, autopilot in your brain cannot turn itself off. It takes conscious effort. So what do we do? We do small, seemingly innocuous things that expose our brains to novelty. Low key, low-risk things help gently coax our logical minds back online so that we can realistically recognize what's important to deal with and what is just seriously irritating.

Small new things are also steppingstones to bigger and challenging new things. But they don't have to be. You are who you are, and your new things are yours and yours alone. Remember those feet on the ground, homebodies, and those roller-coaster fanatics? They aren't the only ones who get to choose how far they stretch their comfort box. Being an introvert or extravert weighs heavily into the new things that you choose. Introverts draw their energy from quiet spaces and alone time and often find loud gatherings draining for too long.

On the other hand, extroverts get energy from being around others and feel drained if they are left by themselves. I am an ambivert--so I love a party. Until I'm done. I'm an expert at an Irish goodbye. Before you know what happened, I'm home, in my pajamas, snuggled under a blanket sipping tea with my dog.

Not long ago, a friend of mine hosted a silent dance party at a local bar. You wear headphones, everyone dances. I thought this sounded like a blast. I shared this event with my husband, best friend, and her husband with the enthusiasm that rivaled a five-year-old girl going to the newest Frozen movie in full princess regalia. And my excitement was met with crickets. Stephanie loves music and parties but hates the thought of anyone watching her dance. Her husband, D.J., would rather die than do anything like this. And Rob was looking for bamboo shoots to shove under his fingernails. I. Was Crushed. D.J. gently reminded me that this was *my new thing*—not theirs. They were always there to support me, but this wasn't the thing for them.

    D.J's and Rob's idea of a new thing is tasting new beers. Lucky for them, St. Louis has no shortage of breweries. This is not my thing. Stephanie loves to find the smallest and most interesting bit of information about old houses that they rehab. Stephanie and I spend hours in old cemeteries and then research the unmarked grave of a Civil War Era madam. That's her new thing. Telling one more lost story of St. Louis.

    If you're an extrovert, it's unlikely that you're going to get excited about researching a musty old house for hours at a time by yourself, although you might. If you're an introvert, that silent dance party probably sounded like torture to you. But you don't know if you don't try. I have found myself doing many things through this project that I never would have seen myself doing before. That's what has made it so magical.

Big Things and Small Things

We get self-conscious when we try new things—what if I look silly? What if people look at me funny? What if I'm not good at it? All of those might be true. But here's the thing. You're probably not good at it. You've never done it before. That's ok. I promise you look sillier in your head than you do in reality, and no one thinks you look funny. Trust me on this. I have a lot of experience to back it up. And finally, if people are looking at you, invite them to join you. I have found this to be the #1 way to get people to stop staring. Explain that you do one new thing a month, and this is your new thing. Ask if they want to join in or take your picture for you. I promise you will have earned a fan.

Stephanie recently told me that she wished she'd written down all of the new things she's done. I think it's easy to take small new things for granted. As humans, we do new things all the time, often without recognizing them. Do those count for the One New Thing Project? That's a good question, and honestly, I think it's up to you. I guess it depends on where you are in your life and what is important for you at that time. At a particularly difficult time in my life, with my illness flaring, I remember writing, "Oh, and my #onenewthing for January? I managed to crack an egg with one hand this morning. Suck it, Julia Childs." I felt so accomplished at that moment when my body and my life felt utterly out of control. I've never managed to do that since, so yeah. That one counts.

Big Things and Small Things

I do have one caveat, though. After nine years of doing new things, I try hard to not make small things the easy way out. My promise to myself was to do one new thing a month. It's amazing how quickly a month goes by at times. Suddenly you're staring down the 30th with no new thing. Several months ago, I did something just to make sure I had a new thing in that month. I didn't get as much out of those experiences as I would have if I had chosen to do them more organically. They felt a bit rushed. And in most cases, the universe handed me better new things within days. It pays to be patient.

If I have learned anything, it is that this journey is not a linear one. I continually check in with myself to see what feels right for me at any moment in time. But what this project DOES do is give you so many more things in your toolbox to know what "right" feels like. It's taught me to enjoy the momentary rapture of eating sushi with your kids, the sound of a singing bowl, and the exultation at cracking an egg one-handed. But more than that, it's taught me to trust myself. It's taught me that it's ok to be both quiet and loud. It's taught me that my choices can be different from others and still be ok. Being able to experiment with that with small things, for me, has been so important.

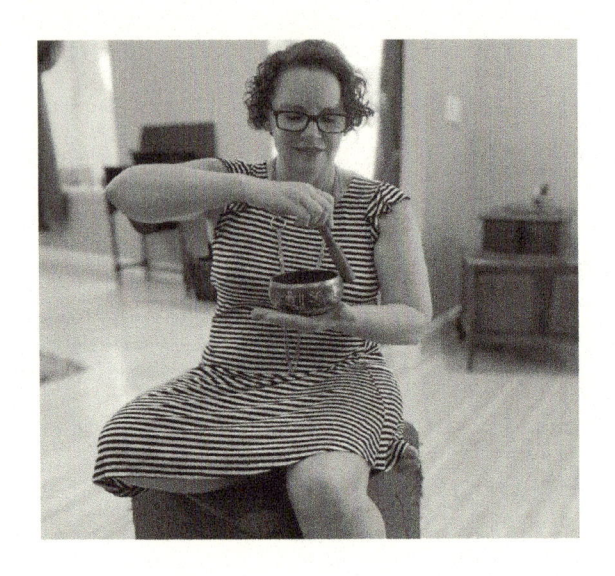

I'm not sure that the project would have been as successful if I had jumped in with both feet into big, bucket list stuff. First, practically speaking, I would have run out of big, hairy, audacious things. It would have exhausted me. But beyond that, the smaller things gave me a chance to learn to trust myself again—to become playful. To fall into the sound of a singing bowl, to savor the taste of the sushi, to enjoy Alex's goading Ryan into trying something we never thought he would touch. If it didn't work, it became a fun story. And there were plenty that would become, as our family would come to call them, "Make Stories Moments." But for now, these small things would help keep our feet on solid ground as we started our adventure.

THE IMPORTANCE OF GROUNDING

Weird Fruit, Finding Your Stride, and Dancing Like You Mean It

I'M NOT WHAT YOU WOULD CALL a science fiction fan. I'm pretty far from a go-to-a-convention kind of a science fiction fan. I like Star Wars, but the original ones. When Jar Jar Binks entered the picture, I was out. Not even Ewan McGregor could save that.

I like Star Trek, but only the Next Generation. The idea of universal peace, a vast array of interesting human-like species, and an omniscient and prankster Q was pretty cool. Plus, Captain Picard was one of those sneaky hot guys that wasn't always looking to bang the green alien girl on the away mission (ahem, Captain Kirk).

Even though I'm not a fan of science fiction, one of my favorite movies is "Passengers." Chris Pratt and Jennifer Lawrence are passengers on this spaceship immigrating to a new planet. They get put into hypersleep for 120 years, but then Chris Pratt wakes up 90 years early because of a meteor. He gets lonely and wakes up Jennifer Lawrence. Blah blah blah, they fall in love. She finds out, moral dilemma ensues, big explosions, and they are about to die. Chris Pratt has to go on a spacewalk to fix the broken spaceship. **SPOILER ALERT BUT TOTALLY WORTH IT FOR THE REFERENCE:** Chris fixes the ship, and just when you think everything is ok, he realizes that the tether to his spacesuit has detached from the ship. He's floating adrift, farther and farther away from the ship. Jennifer Lawrence rushes out to save him, attaching her space suit tether to the ship. She flies out, reaching the end of her rope. Chris continues to drift away, oxygen supply depleted. Suddenly, the end of his tether floats past her hand. She grabs it and tugs, pulling him back. Love story saved. (END SPOILER ALERT)

I love a good love story. That movie was one where I finally got symbolism. I got it in the way that high school English teachers want you to find meaning in the green light at the end of the dock in the Great Gatsby. That kind of symbolism. In

Passengers, Jennifer Lawrence physically and emotionally grounded Chris Pratt. Pretty deep for a 2016 sci-fi movie, right? Experiences that make me feel grounded have always been a part of my One New Thing Project, although I haven't always called them that or even known that that's what they were. I'm drawn to experiences like this when I'm feeling a little frazzled, in moments when my brain can't settle down, and especially when I'm feeling anxious. These experiences are things that are often unplanned. I just find myself doing them because that's what I need.

What is being grounded? We use that term a lot, but it means different things to different people. It can mean connecting with your senses and your body. It can mean pulling simplifying energy from more complex energy. Psychologists define being grounded as completely in control of your mental and emotional state and not being emotionally influenced by things around you. It's easiest for me to describe being grounded in how it feels when you have it and when you don't. When you're grounded, you are sure of yourself, settled. Things make sense. You're calm and unshakeable. You're Neo in the Matrix watching the bullets in slow motion. When you're not grounded, everything feels temporary. You're constantly on edge. You're easily influenced by those around you, and your emotions

The Importance of Grounding

constantly change. It's difficult to focus. You're learning to ice skate and falling down as soon as you get up.

As we grow up, our grounding, or our tethers, is based around other people. Our parents, our families, and later our friends. When I was teaching, I loved being with the babies. As they started to explore the world around them, they would always look back to you just to make sure it's ok. This moment happens right around eight or ten months where they start paying attention to how you react to new things and matching their reaction to yours. I'm sure you've all seen it. The kid that tumbles over and the mom, not wanting a screaming, freaked out baby on her hands, starts clapping and says, "YAY!!!!" Baby looks up, a little confused, and starts clapping and celebrates their fall right along with mom.

Aside from avoiding unnecessary scares for the baby. Playing this time-honored parental game reinforces a biological trick that's hard-wired into all of us. As little ones, we have to know who to rely on to tell us what's ok and what isn't. It tells the baby that the people they trust they are tethered to are good people to let them know if something is okay. That's pretty important for the survival of a pretty cute, soft, wandering little critter with no defenses. That's also the first place they head to when they are sad, angry, or scared. Those adults are the ones that can calm the baby down quickly.

The Importance of Grounding

Those people, first our family and later our ride-or-die friends, are so important to help us figure out what it feels like to feel grounded in the first place—to feel attached to someone or something. It's one of the reasons that psychologists pay so much attention to early experiences. If you have a rocky foundation, it's a harder but not an impossible road later. As much as we can be attached to others, at some point, we need to figure out how to be grounded all by ourselves. At some point, you'll feel scattered, anxious, stressed, or a bit off-kilter. No matter how big your family, or your friend group, no matter how busy you keep yourself, you'll have to deal with it by yourself. Because unfortunately, that's how life is. No one can deal with your stuff but you.

Feeling grounded is a sensation I think we often take for granted. And that's a shame because it's a pretty incredible feeling. It feels tremendous when it's there, comforting, soothing like all is right with the world and you can do anything. Being grounded is a bit like a butterfly landing on you. You have to stop and notice that it's there because it will be gone in a moment if you don't. You'll be left feeling out of sorts—frazzled, going a million different ways, irritable, snapping at people, depressed, maybe stress eating. Yep, I've been there. You don't know quite what's wrong; you just know *something* is. Here's how it works for me: I can usually tell that I'm ungrounded when I have an entire monitor of tabs open, and I have had more than two sodas in a given day. That's one dead giveaway.

One way that I ground myself is to have a cup of strong hot tea with cream. I hold the mug in my hands. I feel the warm ceramic in my palms. I breathe in the scent of the tea leaves. I sip the warm tea and cream. I started drinking cream in my tea when I was a camp counselor in my teens. I worked with several counselors from England--Damien, Kate, and a guy with a complicated name called Nice. They drank their tea that way and teased the Americans for drinking it straight. I've had cream in my tea most ever since, and I think of them every morning when I do. That camp played a big part in who I became. It only takes a couple of sips of tea, and all of those things, including Damien, Kate, and Nice, come back. And then I'm grounded.

Maybe for you, it's going for a run—the feeling of the earth pounding away, mile after mile, your head and your lungs clearer 1/10 of a mile in. Or maybe you find your way to your grandma's kitchen for her secret recipe mac and cheese—the one with the toasted breadcrumbs on top. And as you eat that dish from your childhood and listen to the deep rumble of your grandfather's laugh, suddenly all is right with the world. You are grounded. Tethered. Settled.

When I started thinking about this topic, I drew up a fairly lengthy list of new things that I had done that were grounding for me, but all in very different ways. One of the most surprising ones was star fruit. Star fruit is this little yellow tropical fruit that I first saw in Mexico. I had never seen them before, and I thought they were garnishes. A year or so later, I ran across one at a big farmer's market close to our house. I asked the vendor to pick one out for me. He pulled a pale yellow one, and I went home and Googled how to prepare it. It's simple enough. You cut off each end and then slice away the spines on the five points. Then it's as simple as slicing it just like you would an apple. You're left with are these beautiful one-inch star-shaped treats. They look like they should be perched on the side of the best tropical drink you've ever had, served seaside in one of those beach cabanas with the curtains drifting softly in the breeze and the waves lapping at the sand.

Still, not a fan of tasting new things, I was vaguely suspicious that this thing was far too pretty to eat when I got the star fruit. It's like a scene in a movie where the woman says, "umm. That's the garnish. You're not supposed to eat that," and everyone laughs because, of course, you're not supposed to eat the star fruit, you're just supposed to look at it as art.

There's a slightly embarrassing video of me spending several minutes testing every bit of the star fruit. Sniffing it, testing it tentatively with my tongue, and finally trying a full bite. It was amazing, and I ate the entire thing. I now hunt for star fruit at every grocery store and farmer's market. Not an easy thing to find in St. Louis, Missouri, mind you.

The first one was a little under-ripe, as it turns out. It had the taste and texture of an apple. But it made me unspeakably happy to have found something so pretty and so tasty in my local farmer's market. A few months later, I stumbled on one at a rundown grocery store. I was a little worried that it had gone bad because it was a little darker than the first one I tried and kind of translucent. But hey, I was desperate. This time, though, the taste was completely different. Instead of the crisp snap and mild apple flavor from the first time, the flavor was much brighter—much more like a cross between an orange and a pineapple, but still with a feisty, independent identity, like it was saying stand up and notice me.

    I know, I know. It's a fruit. Even if it's a fun, pretty one, it's a fruit. You're probably asking yourself, "What's the big deal?" Believe me, Rob has been asking me that since I ate my first one. Despite my inability to find them (and I'm truly hoping that my local stores will read this and start adding it to their stock), Star fruit is one of my favorite grounding things. It helps, as the yogis say, to simplify your energy.

    The idea of simplifying your energy is helpful when it comes to grounding. Most of us live with big, complicated, high-maintenance energy. It goes in lots of directions, and at times that makes life a little messy—a lot like a storm or a tornado. It's no one's fault. It's just a matter of having to settle things down from time to time. In nature, we get a thunderstorm. Little kids get to throw temper tantrums. As adults, that's not socially acceptable, although we've all seen people who've done that. We usually don't want our emotional or stressful energy spilling out onto the people we care about, so one of the most effective things we can do is intentionally simplify that energy. Here's how it works with something that's not a star fruit--getting a professional back walking massage. This is the type of massage

The Importance of Grounding

when a trained massage therapist (not your six-year-old or your husband) walks on your back to give you a massage. They hold on to a bar overhead to make sure you aren't getting too much pressure, and they still use all of the massage oil and goodies. It's wonderful for deep tissue massage.

Back to our big, complicated energy - Imagine that your attention is constantly moving to one project, then to an email, then to a crisis, then to who knows what. You're putting out fires and giving all of your energy away. Simplifying energy, grounding in this way, is sort of like creating a giant funnel and taking all of that big undirected energy that is swirling around and directing it down to one very specific thing. You're a bundle of knots, and you can feel yourself ready to snap, so you decide to treat yourself to something different--a back walking massage. As you lay on the massage table, you breathe in deeply and exhale. Your mind goes to where your therapist is working, registering for a moment that her toes are pretty agile at getting under your muscles and releasing those knots. The outer edge of her foot goes right along your shoulder blade and frees it from the tension. You can feel the temperature of the oil and inhale its scent. You can listen to soft music and all of a sudden you get to exist only in your senses.

By focusing on what we can experience through our senses, we give all of that big energy a place to go for a few minutes to calm our restless spirits. Darn those yogis if they didn't know what they were talking about, too. Because it works. It may not be a back walking massage or a star fruit for you. It may be music. A friend of mine throws pottery. You'll find many things that work and some that don't. That's ok. Keep going until you find that funnel.

Maybe for you, it's moving your body. Exercise and movement reduce stress. But there's a bigger reason beyond the neurotransmitters released when we move our bodies to help reduce stress and improve our mood, although that does happen. Certain types of movement change our mindset in different ways.

One of my early new things was to run a 5k. Truthfully, I just wanted to do something that took a little discipline to do. I would use Couch to 5k to run the race, check that one off, take my selfie, and be done with it. Yay me!

I used to say there are two types of people in the world. People who run, and sane people. And then I started running. As many new runners do, I started with the Couch to 5k program. I can unequivocally say that the hardest step was out the front door, especially in cold weather. I hate cold weather. I'd start the warm-up chanting, "I hate this! I hate this!" But by the last set, I'd be chanting, "I'm a rock star! I'm a rock star!" It took a few weeks to get there.

The Importance of Grounding

My best friend, Kathy, with whom I spent many nights at the gym, was decidedly not a runner. So this new thing was a solo one for me, and that made it doubly hard. Or at least it was a solo thing at the beginning. Not long after I started my Couch to 5K, I told my cousin, Misty, about what I was doing, and she was completely on board. The only problem was that Misty lived 300 miles away. We made a plan to train independently, checking in with each other, and then run our first 5k together on Thanksgiving in her hometown of Kansas City.

In retrospect, there were many problems with this plan. We had no idea about how fast each other ran or how to pace a race. However, when I was thinking about bailing on running (and that happened a lot), Misty was texting to see if I had finished my run (a lot of times, she was thinking about bailing, too, I would later find out). I'd begrudgingly tell her no, I was just on my way out, and go do what I said I'd do.

We ran our first 5k on a chilly Thanksgiving morning with both of our families. We both felt a huge sense of pride and accomplishment, which was not diminished by the fact that we were beaten by her husband (a retired Marine, who hadn't trained at all), my 16-year-old daughter (still recovering from ACL surgery), and my 14-year-old son (who not only hadn't trained but was wearing a full turkey costume). But we finished, and that was the goal. Later that Thanksgiving Day, amid pies

The Importance of Grounding

and loud kid card games, Misty and I made plans for our next 5k and a half marathon. We were officially runners.

And run we did. We continued to train together across Missouri--me in St. Louis and here in Kansas City. We figured out the logistics of long-distance training buddies. Each of us with the same Garmin tracking watches so that we could track each other's pace. Our husbands biked behind us on our training runs. They would meticulously map race routes for good spots to stop for a snack for them and to cheer for us, always waiting at the finish line with water and open arms.

Running is a different kind of grounding. It provides a routine structure. The day in and out of training gives you a comforting consistency to rely on. It's the same when you get moving with almost anything. The first part is always awful. At least it is for me. But when I get to the part when my body sort of goes into autopilot, and I feel my breath moving in and out at a relaxed pace, my arms and legs moving in coordination, and my feet on the ground underneath me in a perfect rhythm--one that is just mine, everything else kind of falls away. Simple energy.

Running came along for me at a good time. I was starting to deal with some challenges at work that I had never had before. I felt like I constantly had to defend what I was doing, and I was always on guard. For the first time, I was questioning if I was in the right place. But one of the things that's interesting about running specifically is that runners are less likely to hold on to negative emotions after something happens. They aren't ruminators. I'm a class A ruminator. If something happens, I run it over and over again in my mind--different scenarios, what I could have said differently, done differently, worn differently, you name it. When things started to go downhill at work, I ran over every single scenario in my head—over and over and over. What could I have done differently? What could I have said? Was I just bad at my job? I didn't sleep. I didn't eat. It. Was. Bad. And all that ruminating drove the people that I worked with crazy. It just made a bad situation worse.

Runners tend to not ruminate. They let negative emotions roll off of them like water off of a duck's back. Instead of going over and over something in your mind, you put a pin in it for a bit. Then you can come back to it when the unhelpful circling has stopped, and you can see things from a different point of view that lets you find a solution. I can attest to this happening. I'd finish a run with a more positive outlook (yay for runners high!). I remember getting in my car after even a short run and texting myself how to fix a problem at work that had been bugging me for weeks. And to think, all it takes is a pair of running shoes.

Ok, so you're still on board with runners are crazy. I get it. It's not for everyone. That's what makes the One New Thing

Project fun. You do you. How about dancing? Personally, I love dancing. I've done a few kinds of dancing as part of this adventure, and I still have a few that I want to learn. I need to state out loud that I have no talent for dancing. Absolutely no rhythm. I'm a lot more like a tiny prancing giraffe when I dance. In my mind, I look exactly like Beyoncé. And in the mirror at the gym doing Zumba, I look exactly like someone is giving me electric shock while I fight off an attack of fire ants. Exactly. I can't even do the suburban savior, Country Line Dancing, without getting lost. But, to my credit, I have zero shame, and I love to dance, so I look for every opportunity to go dancing that I can. I've taken Zumba and pole dancing classes. I've done Buti Yoga classes that infuse tribal dance with yoga. I joined a Brazilian dance at a community festival. I even dance in the aisles at the grocery store.

 My favorite of all of these was belly dancing. First, the class was small—six people. Second, ALL of us were insecure. Every. Single. One. Of. Us. There is comradery in that. The type of belly dance that we learned is a pretty improvisational style, so it was also fairly hard to screw up. We learned shimmies and rib isolations, rolls, and arm positions. There were no specific routines to learn, and I have to tell you, that was welcome news to this prancing giraffe. Instead, this style of dance brought us into a circle. Our instructor would begin by

The Importance of Grounding

stepping into the center and performing a series of movements. We'd follow. Simon Says. Easy enough. When she was finished, or when someone else was ready to step in, she'd step out to the circle. Someone else would step in and start a different series of moves. Simon Says would begin again. Sometimes there would be a bit of a lag between leaders, and we would all dance in the circle, using the basic steps, until someone was ready to take the lead. Weirdly, that taught me to be comfortable with silence—to just wait to see what happened and not feel like I had to fill the spaces. I'm still working on that, but those classes started me on that path.

Dance is a completely different kind of grounding activity. By its very nature, it's multisensory--it brings in movement, sound, touch, even smell and sight.

It also has a way of expressing our emotions when words just won't do the trick. All of us, every one of us, has done a happy dance at some point in our lives. You know what yours looks like, even if it's nothing more than stomping your feet over and over. We all know what it feels like--the amazing spontaneity of it. So you, yes, you, are a dancer. It's cool. I won't tell anyone. You can embrace it.

You can enjoy the benefits of dance whether or not you've ever stepped foot on a dance floor. Let's face it, there are lots of different dancers in the world. There are naked in front of the mirror dancers. There are sitting in your chair dancers.

The Importance of Grounding

There are holding your drink, shuffling your feet in line with your friends' kind of dancers. There are conducting the orchestra kind of dancers, and there are bobbing your head in time with the music when you think no one can see you kind of dancers. All of those might feel like me, like awkward giraffes. Our dancing might look different from the pop and lockers, swing dancers, and American Ballet Company Dancers. Still, every one of us are dancers, and every one of us is creative and powerful. If you ever doubt that, dance for one minute.

To some extent, dancing trips our "Am I good enough Switch." And that's where things get a little more complicated. Remember those grounding people? They are super important in how fast we trip our "Am I good enough?" switch. Remember the adorable, squishy, vulnerable baby from a few pages ago? I mentioned that psychologists pay attention to baby's early experiences because if they have rocky ones early, it's harder, although not impossible, to find good people and good grounding later. That's because it's harder to know what to trust. Not getting into too much psychobabble here; think about if that baby keeps falling, and their parent always says "Yay!" or worse, ignores them. Sooner or later, that baby is going to figure out that they are getting hurt, this game sucks, and this person isn't to be trusted. Now imagine the baby is older and they ride their bike for the first time. A real yay moment! But there's no yay

The Importance of Grounding

coming. Or worse, they get told they did it wrong. That makes that "Am I good enough?" switch pretty easy to trip. What's the best solution? Not to try things when it might be flipped *at all*. Especially things that you're not perfect at. So if you think there's a possibility that you're not good at dancing, you're now the worst dancer in the world, that will look stupid, and everyone will laugh at you, reducing you to tears, causing you to wet your pants and run off the dance floor a complete disgrace. All because you danced. Sound familiar? I promise you, giraffe to fellow giraffe. I've pranced in your footsteps, and no one, but no one, is looking at you. Most of us are all worried that we look like prancing giraffes, too. That's ok. Start with small steps. Go from bobbing your head in your chair to dancing in your chair. Move from that to standing on the edge of the dance floor, shuffling your feet in time to the music. You'll get there in time.

There's one other thing that makes dancing unique. Dance allows us to bond as a community. From line dancing to hip hop, from Irish step dance to Navajo ceremonial dance, dance has been used for millennia to tell stories, create a sense of belonging, and create rituals. Our time is no different. Weddings have dance receptions with first dances and father-daughter dances. One of the things that made 2020 so sad is that proms were canceled. Proms are a rite of passage that gives you memories for a lifetime. Cultural dance creates a sense of belonging, of shared understanding of mutual history. It roots us to who we are. The hand movements used in hula and Bollywood speak a language all their own. Hip hop integrated African Dance with tap, swing, and elements of modern dance, for an entirely new style that is rooted in the past but continues to evolve. As a cultural expression, dance allows us to suspend for a moment the feeling of being marginalized, of being rejected, of being others. For a moment, we are together. We belong. Even if we are prancing giraffes, we are the herd of prancing giraffes.

Figuring out how to stay grounded is something that I still work on. I'd love to tell you that I'm this completely grounded person with all of the answers, but the truth is I'm not. I find myself spiraling off a lot. I think that's what it is to be human. I know that in the last nine years, I've added a lot to my

The Importance of Grounding

toolkit to recognize when I'm getting off-kilter faster, and I've added a lot of things to pull me back to center faster. How do I bring that craziness of the world down? How do I suck it into one small, tiny moment? What would that take? A taste of something? A sound? Visiting a place? Maybe a text from the right person. Sometimes that can be my tether.

I think a lot about who grounds me and keeps me tethered. Most of my family has passed away, so I can say that your people don't need to share blood with you with some authority. They just share a piece of your history. And we all have those people. They can be people from your neighborhood, your faith community, or whomever you define as family. When you think you are broken, they are the people that hold you so tight that the pieces come back together stronger than ever.

HOBBIES AND NEVERENDING NEW THINGS

Secret Languages, Music, and Bootleg Booze

ONE DAY IN THE SHEER BOREDOM that lands you on YouTube tutorials, I landed on a "Learn to Juggle in 10 Minutes." Probably a little too optimistic, I was convinced that this was the answer to my boredom. It sounded like it was just my speed. The video was taught by someone who claimed to be a "gold medalist juggler." The juggler was very excited to tell me exactly how to stand with my knees a little bent and my elbows flexed at 90-degree angles, tucked into my sides. Then he demonstrated the relatively easy task of tossing things from one hand to the other. In his case, the "things" were professional, personally branded juggling balls. In my case, they were rolled-up balls of socks, but the gold medalist juggler instructor/YouTuber assured me rolled-up socks would be just fine. SPOILER ALERT: HE LIED. Our goal at first was to toss one ball/pair of socks from one hand to the other in a gentle arc at head level. After about 2 ½ minutes of this, the gold medalist juggler is giddy with his progress. "See how simple that is? Let's move on!" My sock balls, however, started unraveling pretty quickly, flying less than gently between my right and left hand (which right now seems to be attached to a completely different body). I stopped for a moment, realizing just how silly this was. This guy was a juggler. That was his job. Of course, he could do this in 2 ½ minutes. When I did Zumba, I looked like a flamingo on ice skates. I did exactly what I used to tell my 3-year-olds to do. I took a deep breath. And I stopped focusing on juggling. I focused on catching the damned socks. That was it. Tossing and catching the socks.

 I'll be honest. I'm not good at stuff like this, stuff that takes longer than a few minutes to master. I get bored or irritated if I can't master things quickly. I am that gold star kid. I loved getting gold stars as a kid, and I think it's criminal we don't get them as adults. I get a high from checking off everything on my to-do list. I don't even check things off. I highlight them in bright colors so that I can see all of my accomplishments glowing back at me in bright, brilliant color, just like one big glowing smile. I also put way too much on my to-do list, and I rarely get those blacklight-worthy completed to-do lists. I'm great at big ideas like "we should shut down the neighborhood bar for a New Year's Eve Roaring Twenties Party," but that's about where it stops. To be honest, that party only got done because Stephanie has the patience of an angel and the decorating skills of Martha Stewart. I owe that entire one new thing to Stephanie.

I had a boss once who told me that I like to open up the shiny present, but I don't want to put together the bicycle in the box to ride it. That's a pretty accurate description. It's stuck with me ever since, but I've never figured out how to fix it.

Adding hobbies and long-term experiences seems like kind of a no-brainer when it comes to doing new things. How many people say they would love to learn a new language? Or take up rock climbing? Or origami? Looking back through all of my new things over my nine-year experiment, and I realized something. I never picked up a hobby. Not one in nine years.

I had done a couple of classes here and there-- pole dancing classes and such, but I knew they weren't likely to become part of my life. My new things were a lot of fun, and I learned a lot from every one of them, but there's something about a hobby—a new thing with no end date—something that becomes yours and a part of you forever. Now that's intriguing.

Hobbies and Never-Ending New Things

There are some logistical things that go along with doing a hobby for a new thing. When is it done if you never end it? For example, if I'm learning Spanish, do I say, yep, I've learned Spanish when I can count to ten? When I can ask where the bathroom is and not end up in the library? If I'm learning to garden, does it count if I plant the flowers, or do I have to keep them alive for a season? Cause if we're going for B, I'm never going to accomplish the gardening thing. I've killed succulents, and that is a true story.

You can see why someone geared toward checking things off of lists (even if those lists are long and rarely get completed) and getting gold stars would shy away from endless new things. Then there's the problem that hobbies don't end. If I like one and then add on another, I've got two things to find time for on top of a very busy schedule, kids with busy schedules, a husband I'd like to see occasionally, and friends that I want to hang out with. And I'm sure none of them want to sit and watch me learn origami.

Most of us know on a theoretical level that having hobbies is good for us. It's just the practical part that makes them hard. How do I find time for that? How do I spend money on an artist's easel when my kid needs braces? Where am I going to be able to record podcasts? That, by the way, was a real conversation between my husband and me and was something our realtor had to look for during a house search. His request, not mine. We've all got needs, man.

Guys, we all need our time. These particular types of new things can be a very welcome respite in an otherwise busy life. They are your escape—your promise to yourself. And to be honest, it's a great thing to teach to your family. We need to teach our kids how to take time for stuff that they and they alone enjoy—to leave space for it and make it important. And, if you feel like bailing on that promise, remind yourself that learning complex new things that are out of your comfort zone is good for your brain. It helps to keep your existing brain connections and make new ones. It even makes you spry in your old age and wards off dementia. There. You're not avoiding your family. You're saving them from putting you in a home later. Everyone wins.

As much as we agree that adding hobbies and learning new things is good for us and even welcome, the truth is, it's just not that easy to fit into a busy life. To be perfectly honest here, I didn't get to it until 2020, when I was stuck at home for weeks on end with nothing to do. I tried to learn Spanish. *Tried.* I learned to speak Navajo instead. I know. Very relevant in urban St. Louis.

Learning a new language is a pretty common bucket list item, goal, what have you, so that didn't make me special. I talked about learning Spanish since I started the One New Thing Project way back in 2011. Now it was 2020, and with over 250 new experiences under my belt, I was no closer to being fluent in Spanish or any other language than when I had started. Twenty-five years before, I survived Seniorita Anderson's Spanish III class in high school. Back then, we chatted our way through lunch in Spanish, laughing at how American girls said McDonald's and Coca-Cola. Now, middle-aged me, with my foggy brain that rarely used the language, was reduced to the embarrassing "¿Donde esta el bano?" Even then, I was lost when the reply came. I lived in a decidedly Stepford-like neighborhood devoid of people of color. My interactions with people who spoke Spanish were limited to the couple who owned a local Mexican restaurant and the few families who spoke Spanish at my preschool. I wanted my brain to be full and sharp again, and something about learning Spanish seemed like it would make it better. And I truly, truly wanted to begin to break out of my Stepford mold.

But I never did anything about it. I talked about it a lot. I complained that I was far too busy to learn. I complained the apps were far too expensive. Neither of those, however, were excuses for my friend, Stephanie. She learned so much Spanish that when we went to Mexico, she could talk to landscapers who spoke very little English, apologize profusely for her poor Spanish, ask for directions to our building, understand a joke they told, and then get them to give us a ride in the golf cart they had. Then she'd tell me she spoke next to no Spanish. But for me? I just kept talking about it in English.

It took a quarantine and getting to the end of Netflix to decide if I wanted to learn Spanish. When I did, I decided I'd rather learn Navajo. That's right. An endangered language spoke by no one near me. The military used a language so difficult in World War II as a code and remains as the only code to be unbroken.

What happened to the Spanish? It wasn't fun. It became a *should*. I thought I should learn Spanish for a hundred reasons. I *should* learn Spanish because I've always said I would. I *should* learn Spanish so that I could order food at the restaurants in the Mexican district of our city. I *should* learn Spanish to chat with the staff at the resort that we visit every year. But I'd gotten along so far without doing it, and it just seemed like going back to Seniorita Anderson's class all over again to start learning that vocabulary. Did I want to do that? If I need to fit something into a brain that doesn't want to work properly and into a life that is already complicated, do I want to? The answer right now is no. Later that might change, but right now, it's no.

Anytime you're taking on something new that isn't designed to finish, you need to think about how that thing will fit into your life. Whether it's a new job, a new workout regimen, managing your kid's hockey team, joining a book club, or learning a new language, it will take time, energy, commitment, and some brainpower. It will add or take away from the time, energy, commitment, and brainpower going to other things right now. That's why we can't take on too many things at once and why a lot of us feel a hair away from a zombie. That doesn't mean you shouldn't take on longer-term new things. But turn it into another thing on your to-do list? Then it loses its charm.

    I wanted to keep the exquisite pleasure of those small postcard experiences that I'd been collecting. Those moments where you just sort of got lost in the experience. The flavor of words, of the culture, of the experience. Learning Spanish became just learning vocabulary. It became dry, dull, and boring. So I took another look at the app to check out the options. There was a giant list of languages I could dive into, including Russian, Turkish, Irish, Swahili, and Arabic. There were nods to sci-fi fans with Klingon and High Valyrian. And then there were two listed as endangered languages. Hawaiian and Navajo. Navajo jumped out at me. It gave me a Learning an endangered language. Keeping something going. Knowing a little more about a culture that was holding on by its fingertips. Now that was intriguing.

    I got a lot of laughs from my friends and family about learning Navajo. Why on earth would I, on purpose, decide to learn Navajo? I couldn't speak it with anyone. It had no relevance in my daily life. They were convinced I'd learn it only to forget it. I leaned into that teasing and started learning my Navajo. It was my secret language in the middle of the sprawling city.

My mom was drawn to the Navajo culture later in her life. She spent weeks in the New Mexico deserts, camping and visiting the people of the Navajo Nation. She drew deeply on their spirituality during the last few years of her life. That's one of the things that made the Navajo language, and the prospect of being a small part of continuing it so appealing to me. What I did not anticipate, however, was learning so much about the Navajo culture simply by studying their words. They began to tell a tale about how important family is and the importance of mothers. The words relate in sentences share a subtle but deep respect for the world around them and how people are entwined. That's not something that I've seen in any other language—not that I'm an expert—yet.

I started to understand my mom's connection to the Navajo people more fully. Since I was a kid, our big Irish family had a running joke that you were family if we met you once. Holidays at my grandparents' two-bedroom Cape Cod-style house in Ferguson, Missouri, were usually filled with close to 100 people. You waited until you were truly serious with a relationship before introducing them to that insanity, and it always required orientation of sorts.

The women in our family were incredibly strong-willed. My grandmother was called Butch, despite her diminutive stature. The women were known to rally troops for everything from parties to taking care of anyone sick to making sure the 20+ cousins always had babysitters. But mostly, they were badasses before their time. So, it's no real mystery why my mom was so drawn to a culture that honors women.

Hobbies take dedication. They take an investment of time, talent, and sometimes, treasure. And you're probably not going to be great at it when you start. If that's the case, keep going. Keep going until you are good at it. The only thing that matters is that you have fun doing it. That's the only criteria that we're looking at.

In 2020, I picked up two other hobbies. One was playing bass, and the other was making booze. Don't judge on that last one. You know what 2020 was like. It was justified.

It's important to note that I'm not musical anymore. I was once, and I was pretty good. In my all-girls high school, I was one of approximately 47 flutes in our orchestra because that's what Catholic school girls did. You played the flute. One of my friends played a viola and drums and a sax, and I remember thinking how badass that was. I felt for my orchestra

Hobbies and Never-Ending New Things

conductor. How do you find music when ¾ of your orchestra is one instrument?

Rob had a bass guitar languishing in our basement. A friend offhandedly mentioned that Fender gave away three months of online lessons at the beginning of the lockdown. That seemed like a great opportunity to learn to play. I pulled out the out-of-tune bass, a dusty amp, and dug through what we affectionately call the "magic box of cords" to find the right one to connect Rob's old bass guitar to the amp. The first time I made any noise at all, I was like a little kid--feeling all of that sound that I could produce. My son, right down the hall, stuck his head out the door. He glared at me and gave me an incredulous, "REALLY?!" Ryan isn't a big fan of loud noise, much less someone who can't play a new musical instrument well and has the volume turned all the way up. He likes it even less when the instrument has an electrical short and makes pops and screeches at top volume. His Autistic brain was not amused. Fortunately for him, the short gave out pretty quickly, and my initial efforts ended.

Mother's Day rolled around, and I was stuck in my bedroom with my first bout of COVID. I begged and begged for a bass, and my skeptical but obliging family me my very own shiny red bass guitar. It hangs in our office wall underneath Rob's favorite albums, right next to my amp with the cord coiled on top. I follow along with the Fender lessons and sometimes just sit making noise, trying to get my fingers to stretch along the strings on the neck and harden my fingers to the strumming. I still like it turned up to eleven, so I can feel the big thrumming through my body. I suppose at some point, Ryan will get used to it. Or not. Noise-canceling headphones exist, and I had to live through a twelve-year-old him learning the trombone.

The booze, on the other hand, was an entirely different story. At the beginning of the quarantine, we decided to make mead. Mead is a honey-based liquor usually made with berries and some yeast to eat up the sugar of the honey and berries. You pour some water and all of that into a big jug with an airlock and then put it in a dark, cool place for a while until the airlock stops bubbling. The first time we did this, it exploded. Top blown off, berries and stuff strewn over eight to ten feet. I actually had to google how to clean up a crime scene to get that under control. I'm sure that looks great on my search history, but hey, two new things, and now I have a new skill that may come in handy some time. Girlfriends stick together.

Anyway, apparently what caused the booze to explode was a small berry floating upon a bubble into the airlock and clogging it. Oh, and me using far too much yeast. My daughter Alex, being a microbiologist, came over to supervise the next batch. That one went without incident. We called it Six Feet Away from Mead.

When we opened it a few weeks later, we could see thick viscosity on the sides of the glass as we swirled it. We didn't know how to calculate the alcohol content, but that showed that it was high. We took a sip of the unaged mead, called green mead, and confirmed that it was potent. But it tasted good. And a hobby was born.

We got some more supplies so that Rob and I could each make our own batches. Instead of berries, mine would be made with chamomile and vanilla. Mine would also age for several weeks and be opened on my birthday. I called it All You Mead is Love. Rob's was an orange spice version called Mead for Speed. I know, we're clever. He aged his a little less than mine, and it was universally determined that All You Mead is Love was

Hobbies and Never-Ending New Things

a great summer drink, while Mead for Speed was perfect for fall. We were getting better at this.

I'll be honest, it's still not easy to fit hobbies into my life. I'd love to say that I sit on my patio, sipping homemade mead and uttering phrases in perfect Navajo while strumming my bass. There are times I go for weeks, sometimes months, without picking up my bass or looking at my language app, and we only make a few batches of mead a year. Life, dude. Find things that intrigue you, interest you, and pull you in. Don't learn Spanish if you don't want to. To this day, I haven't learned to juggle. I never looked at that video again. Let yourself be a beginner. Let yourself be a three-year-old explorer—collecting information, playing. It takes the stress out of messing up and failing—of being stuck on lesson #3 of playing bass for six months or blowing up your first batch of mead. Make your time for these things special, even if those things only come along every couple of weeks or every couple of months. It's your time. This is your thing. Go play.

HOW TO PROPERLY FAIL

*Bread, Tests, and
Bad Nights at Bars*

IF YOU'RE EXPECTING THIS TO BE a chapter about how to overcome failure, you're probably going to be disappointed. The truth is I don't know how to fail. It's not that I don't fail. I'm just not very good at it. I was that little girl who got the top grade who ruined the curve. And I liked it. I enjoyed it when everyone else glared at me for sinking their grades. I mean, I didn't do it to explicitly ruin everyone's grades, but I enjoyed being at the top.

I played flute at my all-girls high school, which meant there was plenty of room for anonymity. I was decent enough. My orchestra teacher encouraged me to try out for the first chair—the section leader. One of the girls who shared that position played piccolo. I wanted no part of that—playing one instrument, loudly, for the entire audience where any mistake was on display. Nope, it was second chair for me. The music wasn't as challenging, and no one would notice if I missed a note, skipped a rest, or didn't play the correct staccato.

When I was a teacher, I was that weirdo that loved getting my performance review. I knew that I was doing a good job, and it was even better to see it in writing. Better still was to hear your boss, whom you barely saw, say those glowing remarks out loud. Yes, I loved performance review time. I loved getting parent surveys. We had great relationships with our parents, so we always knew what to expect when the results came out. The surveys weren't exactly written to get pointed criticisms. I didn't exactly challenge myself very much, so there wasn't a lot of room for failure to happen. It was a good life. Of course, when you live like that, you have nothing to push you to grow. And that's when the malaise sets in. And that's what led us to where we are today.

At the beginning of my One New Thing Project, I didn't realize how badly I needed to learn to fail. Failure is a curious thing. Humans don't set out to do it on purpose, so it's not easy to learn to do it well. How many of us look at an investment and say, "that looks like it's going to lose all of my money. Let's invest the entire life savings." Do we go out for a walk excited to trip over something? Of course not. That would be insane. Failure, by its nature, puts us in danger, physically or emotionally, so we avoid it.

There are a lot of us perfectionists out there, and our club seems to be getting bigger with each generation. Failure does a doozy on our self-esteem. Even if we're seeking it out on purpose, our brain does an end-around and does everything it can to keep us from failing so that we stay safe. Your brain tries hard to keep you from looking stupid. As a perfectionist, I was not excited about failing, especially at things that I was posting online in front of God and everybody. Those things that had a higher possibility of epic failure kept falling to the bottom of my list—or off of it completely. The world of a perfectionist can be pretty small if you look at it carefully. When I started this adventure, mine was pretty snug.

Here's the funny thing. Failure comes whether you want it to or not, whether you accept it or not. We may not like it. We may not want to call it a failure, and we may not want to face it, but that's what it is. Since it's unlikely that we'll force failure, the best way to deal with it is to figure out how to accept the failure when it shows up.

When I was a school director, part of my job was to hire new teachers. During the interview, I would ask them to tell me about a time that they had failed. One of the most common answers was, "I don't really think of it as a fail. I think of it as an opportunity to learn." After a while, it was hard to keep from rolling my eyes.

Yes, failures are an opportunity to learn. Even the Dali Lama said, "Forget the failure, keep the lesson." But if you can't admit that you failed, you and I are going to have a hard time working together. I recognize the irony of that, given that I have a hard time handling failure. What can I say? I'm a work in progress.

Looking back at the over 250 New Things that I've done, I've had a lot of failures. It's taken me nine years to admit that. I didn't always recognize them at the time, and I absolutely didn't recognize all of the lessons until I could look back through the lens of my memories. Not too long ago, I was interviewed for an article about the One New Thing Project. The writer asked something that I'm often asked. Do I have any failures? For the first time, I said absolutely yes. Usually, my self-esteem saving, perfectionist, self steps in and handles it. "Oh, you know, they all have a great story…" That's completely true. All of my new things have great stories. But some were nothing short of funny, bad, epic failures.

Remember that story about the first time I made mead? Tell me how you make your booze, put it snuggly in your basement to age, and end up googling "how to clean up a crime scene," and don't call that a failure. Great story. Epic failure.

How to Properly Fail

Or the time I made chocolate bowls for ice cream? I used the Dollar Store balloons. They exploded and sent melted chocolate all over our kitchen. You cannot get melted chocolate off of the textured ceiling of a suburban home. It can't be done. It was still there when we moved eight years later. It's a miracle no one was burned. Great story. Epic fail.

Or that time I made sourdough bread? Fifty hours start to finish. My mom made it look so easy. Mine tasted like salty rocks. Definitely a fail. My mom was a rock star--she was a full-time nurse battling depression, and we had freshly baked bread all the time. I couldn't muster one lousy edible loaf of bread. I cried for two days.

Does the fact that I made bread that tasted terrible and didn't rise somehow make me less of a person than my mom? Not really. Bread making was her hobby. I learned in adulthood that it was one of the things that she did to cope with her depression. It also means she had a lot more practice making bread. I also never saw her throw away any bad loaves, but I'm sure there were many as she was learning—her epic fails. I didn't think of that when I stood in my kitchen, apron tied and confident that I was going to finish in a couple of hours with a perfect brown, Pinterest-worthy loaf of sourdough bread that my family would just drool over. Hours later, covered in flour, in my flour-covered kitchen, with nothing but an ugly, inedible, flat lump to show for it, boy, it felt every inch of that failure. It felt like, as a mom, I was failing. As a working mom, I was failing. As a wife, I was failing. All of that was wrapped up in that ugly, inedible loaf of bread.

But what that ugly loaf of bread didn't tell me was that it isn't about the nice warm, delicious-smelling thing I envisioned presenting to my husband and kids like my mom had. It's about all the things that lead up to it, and that can be a monster journey. When I was a teacher, the process of the child's learning was so much more important than the thing they created at the end. That process told us everything about how they thought, how their body and mind were developing and where their hidden talents lie. That's where we, as teachers, could draw new things out of them and help them grow. There are many ways to answer how many crackers we need for five children to each have two crackers apiece. You can count to five twice. You can count to two five times. You can put all of the crackers in the middle and then start subtracting from the pile. It all depends on how the child thinks and if their thinking gives them the same answer consistently.

When we're trying things that are new to us, we're a lot like those kids. We have to learn the right process to make that thing work not just this time but every time. When you're talking about making sourdough bread, many variables go into that. Humidity. Temperature. Whether the yeast has enough flour and sugar to feast on. Someone stomping their feet. Patience. It's very easy to compare yourself to someone that's done it for a very long time and declare yourself a failure immediately, when the truth is, you're just at step #1 of the learning process. As Alexis Rockwell puts it, you're gathering data.

Easy to say, isn't it? But consider this. 50 hours probably isn't long enough for a loaf of sourdough bread, start to finish. It takes 2-3 days just for the first step, the sourdough starter. My mom always had the starter, growing like an alien on our counter or in our refrigerator. I didn't realize the sourdough starter becomes an alien pet of sorts. I do not remember that in any of the recipes, and to be honest, I'm a little salty about it. With their whimsical stories of how the author got into bread making and the long-winded discussions of near orgasmic scents of bread baking, the recipes started with 1. Get you some starter.

When you're baking fresh bread, you have to feed the alien pet pretty regularly--a diet of flour and water so that the yeasties have something to grow on. The starter then gets added in portions to other ingredients--flour, milk, all the good stuff that makes sourdough bread, well, bread. And lots of rising before baking. Being more interested in the pretty golden loaf of bread at the end, I had more or less gone through the checklist for the steps leading up to getting it. Love bread-making. Check. The breeze blowing enhances the scent of what will surely be a magically brown and delicious loaf of bread. Check. Apron. Check. Flour. Check. Eggs. Check. Milk. Check. Starter. Stinky. Let's go.

Had I slowed down and taken time to feed the starter, to treat it as the living organism that it was, not a means to my end, would I have had different results? Maybe. Had I slowed down and taken time with each step of the bread-making--the mixing, the kneading, the proofing, would the end result have been different? Possibly. I imagine my mom found a lot of peace when she went through each of those meticulous steps. She kneaded for a long time. I imagine that was probably therapeutic for a woman with depression in a bad marriage with two teenagers. The bread was just the byproduct.

I haven't revisited making sourdough bread since. Pretty ridiculous, right? It's only bread, after all. I will. But procrastination comes hand in hand with perfectionism and avoidance of failure. That 5th grader inside each of us is good at finding stuff that's a lot more fun to do, even if it isn't logical. My biggest procrastination was well over 25 years. And the thing is, when I finally did it, I failed.

I mentioned that I was a good student. I liked school, and I spent a lot of time at it. When I graduated with my degree in Psychology, my professors told me that I would need an advanced degree to get a job that would allow me to pay the bills. At 22, newly married and working full-time, I started working on my Master's Degree in Developmental Psychology. I had worked full-time through my undergraduate program and was drowning in debt. I was determined to do my Master's debt-free. I worked at an early childhood program in a distressed area of St. Louis City, so I spent my time researching programs to build social skills and reduce aggression with kids living in poverty. I defended my thesis weeks before my daughter was born. It had taken me three years to complete the two-year program going part-time while working full-time, pregnant, and then with a baby. I was exhausted. We all were.

Before I finished my Master's, my professors had cautioned all of us to soldier on to finish our Ph.D.'s. " Don't take a break--you'll never go back," they cautioned. I knew I wanted to get my Ph.D. It was part of the plan, like going to college, like getting my Master's. I liked the idea of those letters behind my name. I liked the idea of people calling me Doctor. It would mean that I had arrived. Finally. Of course, I was going to do it. But right now, I needed a breather. Standing outside the auditorium, wearing my cap and gown and my new hood signifying my Master's Degree, holding my baby girl, I was proud of what I had accomplished. I had been in school for 19 straight years.

I was really, really good at it. I had a great job that I loved. I had a fantastic husband that I only saw in passing when I was in school. I had a beautiful little girl who was walking and talking, and now we had a second child on the way. And right now, I very much just wanted a pause to enjoy it. I was really good at school, and I scoffed at my professors' words of caution. Of course, I would go back. Of course, I would finish those final letters. I even had a plan. Like my Master's Degree, I wanted to make sure that we wouldn't take on any debt for my education. That meant we'd have to wait until Rob and I were a little more established in our careers and the kids were out of child care. That would give us time to save. I also wanted to make sure the kids were older and a little more self-sufficient. Whenever my daughter would toddle up to my office door, it broke my heart when I was going through mounds of research. She'd gently slap at the door crooning "Moooomy..." only to have her daddy scoop her up and say, "Mommy's working now, but we can go play." So, I postponed my return to school until my kids went to elementary school. Or at least that was the plan.

But that five-year sabbatical started to stretch out. I made excuses not to save the money for grad school. Someone needed to do the camp that all of their friends were doing. Someone else needed a hockey/field hockey clinic. We needed a family vacation. The kids are only young once. We needed date nights for us. We needed to replace the small car to fit the hockey bags, field hockey bags, violin cases, and the myriad of friends that now came with our kids. But my professors were right. They all sounded plausible, believable, even. But at the end of the day, they were excuses for doubt.

At the time, I said I didn't have the time or the money to pursue my Ph.D., but the truth is I *enjoyed* being with my kids and their friends. I *enjoyed* spending time with my husband and my friends. I was conflicted. I absolutely loved my work. And I didn't need more letters behind my name to do it. Yet without them, I still felt unfinished, invalidated. The checklist wasn't finished, and the plan wasn't complete. But in the back of my mind, I didn't know if I had it in me to do the work anymore. I was older than most of the students that would be applying. I'd have to take the Graduate Entrance Exam (GRE) again. That test was great at making you feel exceptionally stupid. Lots of math, the kind you only ever need in an 11th-grade classroom and never in real life, and those brain-twisters about which soup are you supposed to have on Tuesday if only 4 soups are offered. I remember the first time I took it, I had some friends from my college in the same test group. We went out drinking after, taking shots of tequila, swearing we'd never have tortilla soup on a Tuesday ever again because of that test.

I didn't get my Ph.D. when my kids were in elementary school. I didn't get my Ph.D. when my kids were in high school, either. Although I talked about it a lot. And I gave a lot of excuses about why I couldn't go back. Instead, I enjoyed my family. I enjoyed my husband. And I built a career that I was immensely proud of. All without a Ph.D. Most people do. And yet, I still had that nagging feeling that something was left undone. So, 22 years after I walked the stage to receive my hood for my Master's Degree, I finally decided to apply for my Ph.D.

Alex had graduated from college with her degree in microbiology and was beginning to look at graduate programs. Maybe that was part of it. At that point in my career, I was on a bit of cruise control. Life at our program was great, but I had been doing this work for 28 years. While I still enjoyed it immensely, it didn't hold the same creative challenges that it once had. Alex was so excited about her future, and it felt good to have that spark.

For her part, Alex was super excited. There was the possibility that we would both graduate at the same time. As soon as I felt the spark, the doubts started to creep back in. I was so unconfident in my graduate school application process that I did not include my application in my One New Thing Project at the time. And this was a huge new thing. I told no one outside of our family. I was even older now--23 years removed from having taken the GRE before. I was 27 years out of that junior year math class. Life had only continued to prove to me that sin and cos had no real relevance in my world--until you had to take a graduate school entrance test. Even now, writing about it four years later, I feel the dread creeping up on me--and I was always the girl who was in the 95th percentile. I crushed tests.

But not this one. Let me tell you, it's a humbling experience to have your college kids teaching you math. But that's what it took. For hours. Years ago, researchers said that lack of empathy was a defining characteristic of Autism. We know now that's not true, and I can tell you I never saw more empathy from my Autistic son than when Ryan made jokes to lighten the mood when he saw how frustrated I got with math that I could not understand. He considered majoring in math, so that must have been as basic as 2+3 to him. On the day of the test, Rob made me a big breakfast with pancakes. Alex and Ryan left me pencils--with a note. "Good luck! You got this!"

I didn't have it. I got the 50th percentile on the math section and 85th percentile on the language section. I was devastated. I used to be so smart. I used to be 95th percentile. Now I was in the 50th? When did that happen?

A few weeks later, I got a call from the education program to which I had applied. They wanted an interview with the selection committee. We were back in the game!

As it turned out, it wasn't my 50th percentile that caught their attention. It was my application and my life's work. I had been a teacher and a school director in wildly different environments, with wildly diverse kids and parents. And I was interested in learning about how kids approached new and novel situations. They asked me which of the faculty I wanted to work with. And that's where it all went wrong. I had no idea what they were talking about. Apparently, in applying for a Ph.D. program, it's common practice to do a little research into the faculty and decide on those with whom you have common interests so that you can work with them. I had missed that crucial step. I felt like an idiot. I was out of my depth.

I wasn't accepted. The graduate school couldn't see past the 50th percentile I got on my math scale and my lack of preparation in the interview. They were concerned that I would not be able to keep up with the math needed for graduate research. As soon as that thin letter showed up, not the big fat packet, I knew. The checklist wouldn't be completed. The plan was over. Failure.

I spent a few weeks telling my family that I was fine and coming clean to my friends about what I had been working on. I was in a bit of a daze. While I hadn't finished that last line of the plan, it had always been there--somehow daunting and encouraging all at the same time. And now, at 44, I put it to bed. I wasn't entirely sure how I felt about it at first. I'd never get those letters after my name.

After a bit, I started to give it some thought. Why had I truly decided to revisit this dream after so long? And here's what that failure told me. I was chasing the dream of someone that didn't exist anymore. When I was young, I thought that the only way I could reach my goals was by getting all of those letters behind my name. When I was in college, I studied psychology because I loved to learn why people behave the way they do. I loved to learn about how children learn and develop. I still love all of those things. They fascinate me. But professors with more years on me told me that the lack of letters behind my name meant I was inadequate. So I got a couple with my Master's Degree. Then they told me they needed more. The truth is, in my career, that MA has only ever been mentioned once, and a Ph.D. wouldn't have given me anything I didn't already have.

Some of the most gifted people I have ever worked with have no letters behind their names at all. What I learned through this process is that although I couldn't recognize it at the time, my life, and my work, had given me all that I needed without any extra letters behind my name. I just needed to let myself be released from that 22-year-old me's plan.

The funny thing about plans is they never quite go the way we expect. When I applied for my Ph.D., I expected to teach at a university and do some research. I never expected that failing at that would open up the possibility of teaching many other things and ultimately leaving my career of 30 years to teach in wellness. My 22-year-old self never would have seen that coming. When you acknowledge your failure for what it is, when you allow yourself to sit with it and give space to it, you begin to understand that your failure exists apart from you. You failed to do something. You are not a failure, and that's a huge distinction. It begins to chip away at the albatross that is perfectionism. Failure is ok. Spoiler alert, the wrong turns can be more interesting than the right ones if we pay attention.

When I tell people about the One New Thing Project, a fairly common question is what is my biggest regret? I'll be real honest. Until 2020, I had no new things that were truly regrets. I had failures but no regrets. Then 2020 hit. And I got COVID. That's a regret. That's my one and only.

How to Properly Fail

I've done a lot of other new things that I probably wouldn't choose to do a second time. I didn't like all of them, like Arak. It's a Middle Eastern liquor that's clear, but it becomes cloudy when you drop ice in it. That part is cool, but it tastes like licorice, which I hate.

Or there was being a hostess in a restaurant for a night. I subbed for the regular hostess at our favorite Mexican place because the entire staff was going to prom. It was awful. People are mean. Tip your servers well.

But there's one story that I don't often tell--at least not all of the details. I hate this story so much that all of the details are only known to exactly three people until now. My biggest fail came from a legendary St. Louis bar. It took me more than two years to recover from it.

St. Louis is known for several things. But at the top of the list are baseball and beer. In St. Louis, you don't so much like the Cardinals, as you're born into it. It was common to watch the Cards on TV with the volume down, listening to Mike Shannon slurring out "swiiiiiing and a miss" and Jack Buck declaring "THAT'S A WINNER" loudly from a scratchy AM signal on KMOX. When Jack Buck retired, it was only natural that his son, Joe, would take over Jack's revered seat.

If you can't be at Busch Stadium with 45,000 of your closest friends, the next best thing is to watch the game with slightly fewer friends and slightly better beer at a neighborhood sports bar. And we take our beer as seriously as our baseball. In addition to the Anheuser Busch brewery, which fills the Southside of St. Louis with sweet hoppy air in the mornings, dozens of craft brewers are scattered across the metropolitan area.

St. Louis proper is made up of 79 neighborhoods, each with a unique flavor. Outside of the city itself, over time, those neighborhoods slowly evolved into 88 tiny townships--just on the Missouri side of the Mississippi--each with their own rules, regulations, and governments. It's led to a distinct form of tribalism that our region has yet to fully confront.

But two things unite us all. Baseball and beer. Unless you're me. It's not something you can say out loud in St. Louis without hearing gasps, but I hate baseball. I mean, I hate it. I've tried. In a town where everything turns red starting in December, I didn't own a single Cardinal shirt until May 2015. Yes, that was a new thing.

All of my friends love the Cardinals. They have husbands' birthdays there. They start talking about Winter Warm-up and spring training and count the days until opening day starting on Christmas. I don't know a single player. And while I usually go to a game or two every year, I generally enjoy the experience more than the game. I love the sun, the Arch over the scoreboard, fireworks every now and again. But to be honest, I find baseball deadly dull.

I'm also not a huge fan of beer. And I have tried. It would have been away more economical hobby in college. With all of the craft breweries in St. Louis (including eight within walking distance of my house), my friends have been on a mission to find one that I like. Sours, lagers, IPA, pilsners, stouts, I've heard about it all. I've tried a lot. But those hops that smell so lovely in the morning taste like dishwater to me. The smell of beer on someone's breath is enough to make my stomach lurch. I've never been able to get over it, and I've tried.

My college was a lot like most colleges. The sanctioned entertainment was pretty lacking, but the parties with free booze were ample. I did what many broke college students do. I went where the entertainment was, and that meant parties with bad beer. If you were lucky, you might get some rail vodka or some Bartles and James wine coolers in a plastic tub. Otherwise, you were stuck with warm beer or Kool-Aid and Everclear—Purple Passion. I was a notorious lightweight, so Purple Passion usually put me on the floor after two drinks. So I tried to learn to like beer. I tried Coors, and Budweiser. I tried Miller and Busch—everything that college kids got for cheap at the Kroger. I couldn't get through even a single one. Not once. Ever. The two-liter bottle of Purple Passion includes "substandard grapes?" I learned to endure that. But beer? Nope.

There you have it. The two things that bring my fractured city together--baseball and beer--and I'm a hockey and vodka girl. Go figure. But baseball and beer are what brought us to a legendary St. Louis bar on a warm April evening in 2011. The bar is called Fast Eddie's Bon Air, and it sits just across the Mississippi from St. Louis city in the tiny Illinois town of Alton. To say that Fast Eddies is a sports bar is a little like saying that Disneyworld is an amusement park. In St. Louis, it's *the* sports bar. Legend has it that the bar has been around since 1921. Fast Eddie's is so popular that they bought the street next to the bar to create a bigger heated patio. As the saying goes, "if you are 21 and in the mood," you head to Fast Eddies. Especially if there is a Cardinal game happening.

On April 2, the Cardinals had just finished a day game. They lost in enough time for everyone to head to their neighborhood bar. Hundreds, like us, headed to Fast Eddies to lick our wounds. This was supposed to be a fairly simple new thing for me—to experience this bar that everyone else in St. Louis (it seemed) had already gone to. Fast Eddie's is a St. Louis landmark, sure, but it's just a bar. How hard could this be?

We planned to meet a couple of friends there. Bob loved baseball. He followed the stats, listened to Joe Buck calling the games, and managed his fantasy baseball team with obsessive attention. Bob also liked good beer. He'd settle for Bud if that's all you had, but he knew good beer and liked to discuss the finer points of hops and such with Rob. Bob's wife, Colette, was born into Cardinal Nation and went to games, but that's about as far as her devotion went. Like me, she was more of a mixed drinks girl, less of a beer girl. Colette and I went to elementary school together. Our husbands were excited to hang out at this cool bar, drink good beer, talk about hops, and try to convince me why baseball is actually a good game. Sounds pretty easy, right? That's what I thought.

It only took a couple of minutes for things to go horribly, horribly awry.

Fast Eddie's is big. I knew that coming in; I mean, they took over the street next to them to make a bigger patio. But it did not feel nearly big enough for the massive crowd that pushed inside. In my mind, it felt like a few thousand people, pushing, pressing, and crushing. As soon as I stepped in the door, I was overcome by noise, bodies pressing into me, and the smell of beer. I couldn't breathe. The walls were closing in. Everything was spinning. I couldn't talk. Even though I was only a couple of steps from the door, I was suddenly terrified that I would lose track of Rob and not be able to find my way out. I looked around wildly for him. Seeing the look of abject terror on my face, Rob grabbed my hand tightly and pulled me through the crowd. I think he said something about the patio. I might have nodded. I don't remember. I clung to him, and somehow, we made it to the patio.

The crowd was just as thick there. People were pressing in on me from every side. There was noise. Noise everywhere. Rob was in front of me, holding my hand, and I remember shutting my eyes and pressing my head against his back, willing it all to go away. I felt tears rising in my throat, and I suddenly felt as if I would choke. I remember being pressed up against a pillar. I don't remember who did the pressing. Rob took my hand firmly and started pulling. My head was still down, but I managed to open my eyes. He pulled me through the crowd to the front door and outside. I leaned up against the wall of the building and was fully and truly hyperventilating. And cried. And still couldn't find my voice. I felt as if I was choking.

Rob wrapped his arms around me and led me back to the car. Bob and Colette hadn't arrived yet. He canceled our plans and took me home. Abort. Rob had the forethought to stop for a picture of Fast Eddie's Bon Air as we were pulling away--a record of my failed new thing.

After that, I developed a crippling fear of crowds. It seemed to develop from nowhere, and it didn't seem to want to go away anytime soon. My family and friends learned to help me with it. During Alex's graduation, Ryan grabbed my hand and ushered me out before the crowd got bad. We left so quickly after the graduates processed out that Rob's parents thought we had gotten lost. Alex got used to waiting until almost all people had emptied from the concert or the hockey game before we left our seats.

The crowd thing stuck around for a long time, but I didn't have a panic attack like the one at Fast Eddie's until several years later. It came out of nowhere, and the circumstances were completely different. I knew these people. I knew this environment. We did this all the time. And yet, there I was. Standing in the foyer of a very good friend's house, I was completely frozen in the middle of our monthly wine club. Barely able to speak. Barely able to contain tears that came from nowhere. Feeling like something is choking me. With only one thought in my head, "I have to get out..." playing over and over on a loop.

Some friends of ours organized a wine club each month to get together under the auspices of learning about wine. Each month had a fun theme--most unique label, celebrity wines, etc. I'm not fancy, so it was a good time to indulge my friend's insistence that not all red wine was like Catholic altar wine. He never won me over, but that's beside the point. The wine club was full of good friends and was an incredibly familiar and fun environment for me. We always came with Stephanie and D.J., who lived just a mile or so from us. But something happened on this night. I'm still not entirely sure what. We had finished with the wine tasting and had moved on to the relaxed, hang out and drink wine portion of the night. That's the part of the night that, if we were all honest, we were really there for. I was talking with a friend of mine, and then suddenly, I couldn't focus on anything he was saying. He must have sensed that something was wrong because he gently squeezed my hand and excused himself. I went to find my husband.

I managed to find D.J. in the crowd. I made my way to him and pressed my thumb into his hand, then left. I contemplated walking the 3 or 4 miles home in heels through bad neighborhoods on the sidewalk outside. It didn't matter. I just needed to get out. D.J. must have gotten the message because a moment later, he had retrieved my husband and Stephanie. They were standing next to me, confused and concerned. As we left, Rob held my hand. Stephanie asked probably a dozen times if I was ok. All I could do was stare out the window. I couldn't speak. Not one word.

It took me some time and the help of a truly gifted therapist to figure out that a) the crowds themselves were not the problem, b) I was not crazy, and c) I did not even have panic attacks. I was having trauma reactions. That new thing at Fast Eddie's that seemed so simple and the wine club years later had one thing in common--lots of alcohol and lots of people in an overwhelmingly loud, way too small place. It triggered memories that I had been pretty successful at stuffing down for almost 30 years--memories of a sexual assault when I was 16 at a party under almost identical circumstances. Until that moment, I had never spoken of it to my husband. And until this moment, I've never spoken of it publicly. For 30 years, those memories festered and left me with PTSD that just helped my decision-making along, so I wasn't in those situations in the first place. I didn't go to the neighborhood bar when it was crowded after ballgames because those were "baseball people," and what did I want with "baseball people" anyway? (I know, I see it now. Therapy helps, y'all.)

My PTSD, as it was officially diagnosed after my panic attack during wine club, reared its ugly head when I started pushing myself into new situations where that part of my brain didn't get to have as much control over decisions anymore. I went to a crowded, drunk, noisy bar. *And then* I went to a wine club where it was also similar to what had happened to me. And then the dominoes fell. I went way too far out of my comfort zone, and my safety feature freaked out. It needed reassuring. It needed help.

It's so tempting after an experience like that to curl up in the fetal position under a blanket and say that you're not going to do new things anymore for fear of tripping those awful feelings. It's tempting. *Very tempting.* Don't do it. There's a Tibetan saying, "When the spring bloom comes, where does it start? Does it start on the hilltops or down in the valleys first? Growth first begins in low places." Allowing yourself to experience the tough times, the failures, the hard feelings allows for great revelations. For me, my revelation with this experience is that my safety feature doesn't need to be dismantled. It just needs to be tweaked. It's my smoke alarm. There are times when it goes off, and I legitimately need to get out of the house. But there are times, like a wine club when it's like I'm making bacon.

That thing is going off all day, but I'm just making bacon. Just wave a broom at it, open the windows, and enjoy the smell.

This experience led to me making an amendment to my guidelines for my One New Thing Project. Try everything twice. Try it once for the experience. If you didn't like it, try it a second time to make sure you did it the best way for you.

I did return to Fast Eddie's. On another warm afternoon during baseball season, our wine club gathered there to say goodbye to one of our own heading off to Afghanistan. I knew the crowd would be big. Huge. Massive. Even so, I wanted to say goodbye to my friend, and with my commitment to trying things twice and reminding myself that sometimes smoke alarms are just for bacon, off I went.

We were hoping to get a seat on the patio. Some people in our wine club knew about my panic attack and my previous experience at Fast Eddie's. Still, nobody knew the real reasons behind them. The only ones there that knew the whole truth were Rob, Stephanie, and D.J. Rob held my hand tightly as we walked through the main room, thumb moving across my hand rhythmically and glancing at me as he pulled me through the crowd. Every now and again, he'd say quietly, "It's ok. I'm with you. Keep breathing." D.J. moved ahead of us to find seats on the patio. They were able to find a couple near the end of the table where it was a little less crowded. Stephanie and I sat down.

Our husbands positioned themselves behind us so that passersby didn't press in on either of us. Every now and again, Stephanie would gently reach out and touch my hand. I let out a very deep exhale. Although it didn't entirely go away, the smoke alarm in my head quieted, and I could focus on the other people. I remember the conversation. I remember talking about baseball. I remember people teasing me about how I was the only person in St. Louis that didn't like it. I remember tasting the beer. It hadn't improved since college, but I tried.

    Our bodies and minds are not meant for failure on purpose. However, failure does us a lot of good. It's where we grow. When muscles fail, that's when they come back stronger. We're the same, if we can learn to approach failure as a moment to learn, to collect information, to explore, and regroup. It teaches us strength, it teaches us perseverance, and it reveals who we are--but only if we let it. Failure is good. Failure allows us to strip away what isn't working and try something else, as long as we dare to face failure head on for what it is.

    Changing my guidelines so that I do failures over has been a good thing for me, and there are few failures that I need to revisit. I don't keep going back if I fail more than twice. There's no sense continuing to bang your head against a wall trying to turn it into a door. That new thing may not be for you. Baseball and beer will never be as much fun as hockey and vodka. Sorry. You'll have to fight me on that.

It is important to recognize that every experience--every failure gives us new information to build on. I became a much different person after I realized that the process of doing something was just as important as the end product--something I had been teaching young children for years. Messing up that stupid bread so badly made me understand everything my mom was going through when I was growing up—a time when we had a strained relationship. It gave me a lot of respect for the woman who raised me during a very difficult time in her life. I don't know that I would have had that without making that ugly bread. If I hadn't failed at getting into graduate school, I would not be where I am today—the owner of two businesses. And I would be much less happy and a whole lot less healthy. If it weren't for a bad night at a bar, I would never have realized how much I avoided without even knowing it—how much of my life I wasn't living. I wouldn't have realized how truly strong I am and how much the people around me love and support me. Yes. These were failures. Huge, glaring, epic fails. But by staring them square in the eye, not blinking, and seeing them for what they are, prepared me in no other way for who I am now, and more importantly, what would come my way.

How to Properly Fail

SHAKING IT OFF

Beads, New Gigs, and Giant Grasshoppers

CROWDS ARE STILL HARD FOR ME. My eyes still dart around for the exits. Everything still feels very amplified—the sounds, smells, and slightest touch from a stranger moving past feel like a mob crushing in on me. I'm constantly watching for the people that I'm with. My greatest fear is that I'll lose the people that I've come to within a sea of tens of thousands. How would I ever find them? And yet, I still go to concerts. I still go to hockey games. I still go to festivals. I've figured it out. If possible, I stay on the fringes of the crowd, and if that's not possible, I hold on to someone's hand. They walk in front, and I walk behind. When we go to a restaurant or a bar, I usually request a booth because it's easier to hear and people can't walk behind me. If not, I'll take the seat where there's less traffic. I almost always have earplugs with me if I'm in a place that gets too loud, and I always always have sunglasses. Most importantly, I'm pretty open with the people I'm with about what I need when I'm in situations that may give me trouble. And for the most part, it's worked, except this one time.

St. Louis throws a massive Mardi Gras festival. As you might guess, our Mardi Gras comes with all of the requisite drunken debaucheries that you would expect from a week of sinning in preparation for Fat Tuesday that gave the festival its name. It's the kind of party that makes for a good confession on Ash Wednesday that ends with a smudge on your forehead and a priest giving you a half-smile while he sort of shakes his head at you. That's a look that only someone who was raised Catholic can know.

I'd been to Mardi Gras two years prior as a New Thing. It was bitter cold, so the crowds were as subdued as they could be with a thick liquor blanket. St. Louis Mardi Gras is held in Soulard, the city's oldest neighborhood. An area originally made up of tenements that housed poor French and German immigrants, Soulard has a rich history and is now one of the trendiest places to live. St. Louis Mardi Gras has grown to the second-largest Mardi Gras celebration in the United States. We're second only to New Orleans. That's kind of a big deal when you compare the space that we occupy against the space in

New Orleans—just a few square blocks. Although most of us think of Mardi Gras as a booze-filled blowout (and it is), it lasts for weeks in a real Mardi Gras city. Mardi Gras begins with Twelfth Night in January and ends with the Mardi Gras Grand Parade the Saturday before Ash Wednesday. In between, St. Louis hosts a family winter carnival, a Bacchanalian Ball, a Cajun Cook-Off, the requisite 5k, a restaurant tasting, and bar crawl, a pet parade, a wiener dog derby, and the Mayor's Mardi Gras Ball. There's a lot.

The first time I went to Mardi Gras, it was well before the epic fail at Fast Eddie's. We still lived in our suburban utopia, so going to Mardi Gras meant getting up early, driving the 45 minutes into the city, hunting up a parking place in the reserved section with a special pass, thanks to our friend, Bob, who lived in the area, and walking several blocks to the parade route before things got super crowded. As a result, we got to the parade route about two hours before it was supposed to start. It was cold, and the streets were already filled with drunk people. We got some hurricanes, found a spot, and enjoyed the people watching until the parade started.

It's weird how competitive you get for cheap beads. As the alcohol flows, one of two things happens. You either see everyone as an enemy, or you see everyone as a friend. I'm generally the latter. Since Kathy and I had been standing in the same place for several hours, we got to talking to the people around us, and we formed a sort of bead gang. As the floats threw strands at the crowd, taller people snagged them. If they landed on the street in front of the barricades, Kathy and I, being smaller, would shimmy underneath and retrieve them. We'd compare our booty and trade our plastic jewels. About 3:00 that afternoon, with the last revelers heading to the bars, we made the long trek home exhausted, with several inches of heavy beads piled around our necks. It was a good day.

So, when we moved to the city several years later, a mile or so from the neighborhood that hosts Mardi Gras, Rob and I were pretty excited to be able to go. There wasn't going to be the hassle of getting up early and driving. Gone was the problem of finding a parking spot. We didn't have to stay any longer than we wanted to. We could come home when it got too rowdy and eat pizza at our local bar. Winner, winner.

It was 2019, four years after the Fast Eddie's debacle, when we went back to Mardi Gras. It was a beautiful 55-degree day in March, so it felt like 2/3 of St. Louis showed up for beads and booze. As planned, Rob, Stephanie, D.J., and I walked the mile or so from our house to Soulard. We planned to meet up with a bunch of other friends on Russell and Broadway, next to the parade route. Apparently, 500 other people had that idea, too. It quickly became apparent that the possibility of finding our friends there or, quite frankly, trying to call or text them was laughable.

We abandoned the thought of trying to find our friends for the time being and went in search of more quiet surroundings on the edge of the crowd. The sound of the crowd was becoming disorienting, and I was getting a little dizzy. As we moved through the crowd, I stepped up to a platform and fell. Hard. I got back on my feet, but my hands and knees were covered in blood. I shook it off and wrapped up my hands in the sleeves of my sweatshirt. We kept walking, with me holding onto a hand in front of and behind me until we finally made our way to the thinner parts of the crowd.

A little while later, I realized I didn't have my phone, which also contained my ID and a credit card. Stephanie called it, and fortunately, a Good Samaritan answered it. He gave her a pretty good idea of where he was and said he'd wait for her.

Shaking It Off

She turned and took off in pursuit in a near sprint. Not wanting to get separated, I followed her. I turned around and saw D.J. behind me at a distance, with Rob behind him. When I turned back to Stephanie, she had turned a corner and was gone. I lost her. I stopped and turned back to find D.J. He was lost somewhere behind me in the mob with Rob somewhere behind him.

It had happened.

I was lost in a sea of hundreds of thousands of people and was completely alone. I had no phone. I had no way to get in touch with my people. They were separated and impossible to find. I was paralyzed.

For a few moments, I just stood, trying to collect myself. The crowd pushed in toward me. The noise got louder and louder. It got harder to breathe. I felt the tears coming. I compelled myself forward, in the direction that Stephanie had gone, looking for the edge of the crowd. I didn't stop until I felt the fresh air and the metal of the barricade. I took great gulps of air and tried to hold back the panic. A man standing a few feet away from me must have sensed something because he took a step forward and gently asked, "do you need any help?" All I could do was shake my head no, but I couldn't make any sounds.

He moved back to his place against the barricade but continued to keep an eye on me. And that allowed me to take a breath. Slowly my mind began to clear. No, I didn't have a way to find my people, and yes, there was a whole city of people in front of me. But if I walked straight forward, I would end up back at our pub. And there, people could help me. So that's what I resolved to do. I nodded to my helpful stranger. I took a deep breath and concentrated on putting one foot in front of the other. I had been walking for about a block, and Stephanie miraculously appeared in front of me in the crowd. She grabbed my hand and pulled me to a side street where Rob and D.J. were waiting. I grabbed Rob and held on to him. I knew I was safe. And I knew that I had handled myself just fine.

I wonder what I would have done in that circumstance had I not returned to Fast Eddies years before. That one act, and many after it, gave me what I needed that when put to the test, I could choose how I responded. There's a lot of power in that—being able to choose our response. It means that we can move forward and that our past doesn't own us. We're resilient, learning, growing humans. And that takes the sting out of failure.

Being resilient means that we can adapt. Especially when the rubber hits the road. It helps us to move forward. I am so much more resilient for doing new things. At this point, I've done so many new things that I expect to fail at most things the first time I do them. I've made a lot of recipes during my project. I'm still a pretty awful cook. I routinely mix up teaspoons and tablespoons. That's a pretty big deal when you're talking about chili powder. It does not, as my husband tries to tell me, give it a little more "zing." In Ryan's unedited words, what it does is make the entire dish "completely inedible."

However, I am a much better cook than when I started out. I know, for instance, that I am a novice, and there is no shame in that. That's important to embrace because if you're doing an unfamiliar recipe, especially a complicated one, it will probably have unfamiliar terms and equipment. Read it first to be prepared. Also, it will always take you longer than the person writing the recipe. They do this all the time. They are good at it and generally don't screw it up. I need to plan for screw-ups. That's going to add time. I bring all of this up because my fragile little ego has been bruised a lot by lopsided cakes, burnt casseroles, and gooey desserts. Spare yourself. These things are not you. They are things that you do, but they are not you. Remember, you're gathering data.

What does trying a new recipe have to do with the secrets of life? You do little things so you know you can accomplish big things. We practice overcoming small failures to be brave enough and crafty enough to overcome the big challenges. And those big challenges always come, whether we want them to or not. I could have locked myself away and avoided all of the crowds in my city, but that meant I denied myself a big part of what made my city the amazing place that it is—concerts, festivals, and yes, Cardinals games. I love my city, and to fully love it was to love all of those things (I still just love Cardinals games for the experience, but we'll call a truce on that). I didn't have a choice when Rob got laid off, and we had two kids and a mortgage. We had to figure that out. And we did. Because we'd already learned that we could do hard things.

I was not good at failure. But what I was good at was solving problems. It never occurred to me that those two things were one and the same, at least not until I started looking at failure as collecting data. And that, fortunately, is something that I am good at. When you fall on your face, you have a choice. You can stay there, or you can figure out what tripped you and fix it. Sometimes you need help with fixing it.

To make any changes, we need to have a realistic understanding of our choices at any given moment. Stress often makes it feel like those choices are artificially limited or that there is a lot out of our control. That's our survival brain trying to help us out—by limiting our vision to critical things. But in doing that, it often misses out on some pretty big opportunities. That's why having lots of experience helps. It makes you a little more comfortable in those circumstances when your survival brain starts trying to shrink your choices. You have a lot of things in your tool belt to choose from. You have already solved a lot of problems, so there's no reason you can't solve this one, and you've already shown yourself that you do hard things.

2017 and 2018 were filled with these kinds of new things for me. My illness was progressing quickly. I had blinding migraines every day. My office was kept dim, and I could only work on my computer for about 20 minutes at a stretch before doing some stretching and yoga. On top of that, I had full-fledged attacks, with numbness, confusion, and other disturbances about 25 days a month. I missed visiting the kids and the classrooms but the noise and lights triggered symptoms. I'd have to go into a dark and silent room for hours afterward. I hated it. I knew I wasn't doing a good job, but I couldn't quite let it go. I loved everything about what I did. If I wasn't a teacher, if I wasn't running this school, what would I do? The thought gave me such depression that it brought me to tears to even think about it.

Unbeknownst to me, my friends and family had been discussing the effect of my work on my health for months. They just didn't know how to bring it up. When they finally did, I was prepared with a well-thought-out, reasoned, impassioned argument with exhibits about how there was no way that I could leave my job. My income was a big part of our family budget. My illness was manageable. I loved my job. *I don't have much of a choice.* And then my friend D.J. spoke. He was characteristically blunt. "That's fine. But you'll be dead of a stroke in a year."

Sometimes you need gentle, sometimes you need blunt. Know when you need which. I needed blunt.

What I needed, and what many people who are resilient need, is someone who cares a lot about them to help them see what needs to be changed, what can be changed, and help find the difference between the two. Rob was that guy for me.

To understand the difference, imagine you are on a small boat in a storm on the ocean. There are several things that you can and need to do. You should probably do some good steering and safety protocol. You can also change the music that's being played or change your shoes. Probably not the best time for that. You might also think you should learn to captain a bigger boat. That's also great, but not going to help in this circumstance. You'll have to get a plan for that after you're out of this crisis.

I was constantly in that small boat in the storm, tossed around. And I was changing my shoes while trying to steer. It took someone who was outside the storm to lash onto my boat and pull me to safety. My husband opened up choices that my survival brain had previously closed. He suggested that I look at getting my yoga teacher certification—I could teach yoga to kids if I wanted. My friends helped me see what my choices were. In reality, those distractions—those things that I could do but wouldn't ultimately help me get to what I wanted.

Of course, there were many other reasons that I was scared to leave my job to be a yoga teacher. I had been in my career for over 30 years, and I was good at it (although not so much lately, if I was honest). I was 46 years old. I had this disease that was controlling every aspect of me. I wasn't exactly what you think of when you think yoga teacher. I was not young. I was not thin. I was not Zen. I'm DEFINITELY NOT vegetarian. Seriously, who the F would want me as a yoga teacher? I also curse a lot. It seemed like that wasn't a great attribute for a yoga teacher.

But here's the thing. If I did this big scary thing, quitting my 30-year career to be a different kind of teacher, and fell flat on my face, what was the worst that would happen? I'd have a yoga certification that I could use and maybe keep myself a little healthier. Financially, we'd have to tighten things, but we'd be ok. Best case scenario? I could have a new business with a lot more flexibility. If it didn't work, I could just stop doing it. One more new thing under my belt.

So, I did it. I quit my job, letting go of those 30 years, but holding on to the skills that they gave me. How to work with people, take something that I'm teaching and tweak it for just one person. I got my yoga teacher certification. It turns out that there's a lot of people who want a yoga instructor who isn't young, or thin, or vegetarian, and maybe even curses a little. I've failed a lot along the way (can we talk 2020?). And I've collected a lot of data. I've changed many things, and I've kept many things. I've cried a lot, and I've drunk a lot of wine. And through all of it, I've kept talking to other people—because your people help you see solutions when you can't see them yourself. They see your strength when you can't find it yourself.

Staying resilient and open to change isn't easy for most of us. I find it easier if it's approached with a sense of optimism and humor. Of course, it's easier to do that if you've got a little experience at trying New Things and having them work out for you, or quite frankly, trying new things and having them not work out, but being able to get a good laugh out of it. Like that time, a bird-sized grasshopper landed on me when we were in Mexico. I kept trying to tell Rob to get this thing off of my back. He and his best friend did their best to convince me it had landed on a post nearby while that bastard moved to the front of my dress and dug in. I stood there frozen until Rob and D.J. spotted it deeply embedded in the front of my dress. Rob tried to swat it away, but that giant grasshopper was holding on for dear life. D.J. pulled it off, pulling half of my dress with it. He walked down the corridor with its ugly little head poking out the top of his hand and its wings sticking out the bottom. Stephanie, who is absolutely terrified of any bugs, was none the wiser. I told her about it later, and she said, "Oh my Gosh! You are my hero! I would have ripped all of my clothes off!" I looked at her and said, "I was completely catatonic." She burst out laughing. Yes, giant grasshoppers prepare you for bigger things. I promise.

Our family went through a lot of changes since I started the One New Thing Project. Two high school graduations, two kids in college, two college graduations, and trading in our suburban home of 23 years for new urban digs. And that last one was tough.

Rob was working at a Fortune 500 company in the city. For 24 years, he commuted for anywhere from 45 minutes to over three hours, and he had about had it. My yoga classes were bringing me into the city more and more. We found more to do in the city after work—independent restaurants, funky places to hang out, and festivals--things our little bedroom community just didn't have.

One day, I got a phone call from someone asking if we'd be willing to sell the house. They were looking to flip some houses in our neighborhood and couldn't find anything they liked. They took a shot and called me on our ancient landline.

Were we interested? I named an outrageously high price, and they took it. Our pie in the sky discussions about moving to the city was suddenly very real with that call.

Both of our kids still lived with us. Alex had just graduated from college and was working in the city. She hated the commute, so she was an easy sell. Ryan was still at college. He was decidedly less happy about the prospect of us selling the only house he'd ever known. Knowing we were about to break the news, Alex winked, "Good luck with that!" and dashed out the door, attempting to avoid the scene. While she didn't avoid Ryan wailing "WHYYYYYYY?????," she did miss out on his 30-minute dissertation on why we could not sell the house without his permission. We sold the house anyway. Ryan moved, and now he says he'd never go back to our old community where he can't walk to the corner store.

We settled on a city home a few doors down from a pub that we had fallen in love with years before and a mile or so away from where I had grown up. Once we found our new place, Alex and Ryan got to decide on their bedrooms—both located on one floor away from us. Ryan got to pick the internet service (it's his major, and he's way better at that). They also decided what they brought with them to the new place and what to leave behind—with some caveats. Ryan isn't sentimental and would have been just as happy to pitch all of the baby stuff we had kept in his closet. Instead, Alex went through each item with him and packed it, leaving a single box in the middle of our kitchen marked "Ryan's Sentimental Bullshit" in large block letters on the top of the box.

The same way I approached my career change, we approached our move as a new thing. It was a new adventure for all of us. But at the end of the day, if we hated it, if we hated the house, the city, anything about it, there were other neighborhoods and other houses. And this would be another story of the multitude that we were collecting. And so far, we have collected many new stories in our new home. All of us, including Ryan, have fallen in love with our new surroundings.

The One New Thing Project is great at many things—helping you figure out what cool things are in your city, helping you figure out what you are good at, helping you expand your comfort zone, and take risks. But wrapped up inside all of that is this—figuring out how to fail with grace. Not fail upward. Not fail forward. None of those euphemisms that try to sugar coat failing or make it something that it's not. Failing is awful. Failing sucks. Change is terrible. It disrupts our normality, and that makes us uncomfortable. This project teaches you how to be resilient. It teaches you how to try things, try them again, and again if necessary. It teaches you that if something doesn't work, it's just a thing that you tried. And you got a good story out of it.

GETTING CREATIVE

Jazz, Gingerbread, and Bold Strokes

I NEVER REALLY THOUGHT OF MYSELF a creative person, at least not in the traditional sense. I don't paint. I don't craft. I don't play instruments. If I have to be honest, coming up with over 250 different new things inspires a certain amount of creativity just by itself. At the beginning of the project, I had a hard time finding new things to do. Now they just seem to pop up. I find them all over the place. I have a running list of things that sound interesting to investigate, to try, to hunt up. I have things that I want to do in the summer that I only think about in the winter (kayaking doesn't sound like the most fun

Getting Creative

thing to me in the winter, but if that's your jam, you do you). I have cool ideas to do by myself. I have fun ideas for date nights. I have ideas that are only interesting to Alex and me or might only be good girls' days for Stephanie and me. I also have some things that would be awesome for a big group of people. This part of my mind is like a faucet that I can't turn off. The moral of the story? Doing new things=get more creative=doing more new things. You get the idea.

I'm obsessed with all things creative. I binge-watch Project Runway and Netflix shows about glassblowing and metalsmithing. The act of creating something that didn't exist except inside of your brain is absolutely fascinating to me. I think I'm obsessed with all things traditionally creative because I feel like I have to work harder at it. Those things don't come easily for me. I have huge respect for creatives who put it on the line every day—their heart, soul, and everything for the world to judge. You paint, hoping to not live as a starving artist. Your band plays awesome music in trashy clubs hoping the right person will finally hear you and give you the right shot. You write a book hoping it doesn't get lost in the cavern of Amazon anonymity. Creating is hard.

Creating is natural when we're little. It's unbridled. Want to be Elsa for a day? You're Elsa for a day, full princess costume and all. You answer to nothing but Elsa. One of the very coolest things about working in early childhood for as long as I did was that I was included in these flights of fancy for hundreds of kids on hundreds of days. I had a tiara in my office because, on some days, I was called into action to be the queen. One day I walked into a suspiciously quiet prekindergarten class. You should always be a little nervous when twenty four year olds are silent. A little boy stood up with a roll of toilet paper and said, "We're in Egypt, and you get to be the mummy." For over an hour, that entire class wrapped me in toilet paper bandages. What can I say? Sometimes you're the princess, sometimes you're the mummy. It did get me out of a meeting with my boss, though.

Kids are inherently creative. Their creativity cannot be contained. It oozes out of them, sometimes into imaginary friends, sometimes into crayon murals drawn on the walls. As we grow up, our imaginary friends disappear, we stop talking to our dolls, and those big bright crayon murals get redirected to smaller pieces of paper to save walls. Our big, bright expressions of self all of a sudden become tame—and turn into pictures that look just like everyone else's. Sunrises start to look alike. Trucks only differ in the number of wheels or their cargo. Flowers vary just by the color of the petals. We give up a bit of our creativity for approval and the comfort of fitting in.

Here's how it starts. As we're drawing those cool multi-layered things, full of story and character and whimsy, people

Getting Creative

start to subtly give us clues about what is good and what isn't. You might get a "that's a nice picture" while someone else gets "wow! That's awesome." We start to get an idea about what gets approval and what doesn't, and we move our creativity in that direction.

Here's the problem. More often than not, the "wow! That's awesome" kinds of things are only "wow! That's awesome" because the people judging them already understand them. Your interesting way of doing math isn't the way it's taught. Your story is weird. Your music sounds like noise. None of that means you're not creative. It means that the world hasn't caught up with you yet. We rarely talk about those outliers, and we rarely acknowledge how unique they are. Outliers are where true creative genius lies. If everyone could do it, they wouldn't be on the fringes.

There's a lot to be learned from the creativity that doesn't jive with yours—to challenging your perspective of what's creative and what's not. When I was young, my dad made a valiant effort to understand the music that I liked. I was an 80's kid, so this was in the time of gender-fluid icons like Boy George, Michael Jackson, and the Eurythmics. Sitting in his recliner, my dad listened to Boy George and remarked, "She's not bad."

I rolled my eyes and said, "Dad, that's a guy." Later, Annie Lennox took the stage in early Elvis Presley style. My dad sat up. Elvis was his guy.

"Elvis is back in style? Guys are dressing like that?"

"Dad, that's a girl. Guys can dress like girls, and girls can dress like guys. It's no big deal." He studied me for a moment, willing his conservative Catholic mind to understand. Finally, he shook his head, sat back, and smiled.

Two years into the One New Thing Project, I found myself in my dad's shoes. I hated jazz. To be honest, it sounded like four people playing different songs, all starting at about the same time and maybe ending around the same time. To me, it was nothing but noise. Rob, on the other hand, loves jazz. He and my grandfather had a very special bond over it that I never quite understood but always envied a little. Rob suggested that we go listen to live improvisational jazz at a small bistro in the arts district. It was my first time hearing live jazz off of Bourbon Street. I was skeptical about the music, but I got to wear a pretty dress and have a nice night out, so I was game.

The bistro was an upscale place with a speakeasy feel. We sat at cozy tables with low lighting. Four men took a tiny stage and picked up their instruments—a rotating assortment of brass, string, and percussion. Each song seemed to hold its place in time suspended. The musicians would begin, and then the group would quiet, and one player would move to the forefront in a solo. One after the other, moving in and out of the song seamlessly, picking up the main rhythm in between. Each song ended with the group returning to the song's backbone, ending exactly at the same time. Each piece was completely improvised, always walking on the edge of chaos and then stepping back. Gone was the noise that I heard before. This was magic.

Leaning into that chaos—to the things that don't initially make sense to us is important for our creativity. It's in those moments of discomfort that we become keenly aware of things that need to be fixed, of problems to be solved, and of new ideas to be birthed. If we too quickly from our discomfort, we may not get the chance to see the opportunities within the problems that lead to new innovation.

And that's where trying new things comes in. Trying new things lets us become more and more at ease about sitting with things that don't feel good. It lets us begin to understand why we don't feel comfortable so that we can do something about it that might make a lasting change. It lets us begin to challenge the status quo, and that is what true creatives do. True creatives make new and better solutions for existing problems or maybe for problems that haven't even been thought of yet.

Creativity comes from being able to sit in uncomfortable situations. We're not often pushed to be creative unless something needs to be changed. To do that, we need to figure out how to do the very thing we don't want to do—get uncomfortable. That's where doing new things comes in. New

Getting Creative

things push us gradually out of our comfort zone while feeding us new perspectives and new ideas that we can use.

Even with just a toe, stepping into your discomfort is a big step toward a much bigger world. It's in that tension that creative magic happens. We recognize that something needs to be changed to fix the discomfort. When we encounter new things and feel that tension and then navigate them successfully, we get a rush in the happy centers of our brains. That makes us solidify the memories and makes us want more of that feeling. That begins to open us up both to newer things and more creative lines of thought. If you're an artist, you may explore different media to work with. You step into a dance class and begin to feel surer of yourself. That carries over to work, and you feel more confident in your next presentation.

Ok, tap dancing can help with a budget presentation? Yes, but I sense your skepticism. The important thing is that you are doing novel things. Some of the most innovative people on our planet have probably never picked up a paintbrush in their life. When we do new things, it primes us to start looking outside the world for the next cool new thing we can do and more internally for the next cool thing we can do. What's the next challenge? What could be another solution? Is there a new project to take on? That's when things get interesting. That's when creativity on all levels begins to happen. We start to see patterns and opportunities that didn't exist before. We stop drawing boundaries in our brains and start making connections. You can pull a little from column A and a little from column B in your mind to figure something out. I often draw on my experience working with young kids as well as my experience as a chronically ill person and the times I had to talk a parent through nerve-wracking times with their kids as I start designing a yoga practice for a new client. Column A, Column B.

When we are pulling information from different places in our mind and looking for new opportunities internally, our brain's happy centers are getting a lot of input, both from external new experiences and now from our internally created new things. It begins to create a feedback loop—do new things, jazz up our brain, our brain does cool new brain things, we want to do more new things, and it starts again. The by-product is lots of creative juice. We give back to our brain just by being our best creative, tiara-wearing, superhero selves—by letting loose and letting our creativity go.

Here's the other cool thing about doing new things. When you do new things, it lights up all of the happy buttons in your brain, making you want to more new things. When you do new things, you can't rely on your old habits and patterns to get you through. You have to consciously think about what you're doing. There's no autopilot here. It makes your brain do some work. When you go back to the regular old run-of-the-mill problems that you need to solve, your brain is now hyped up and ready to work—it's alert. And that helps you be more creative and solve things in new and different ways. It frees you from the "we've always done it this way" trap. The more new things you do, the more practice you have at many different kinds of problem-solving, and the better you are at it. It's one reason doctors have said for years that one of the best ways to hold off dementia is to change up your routine and try new things. Keep your brain moving.

I built my first gingerbread house as a part of the One New Thing Project. We'll just move past the fact that I was well over 40 before this happened. My school did a gingerbread house contest. Each classroom or department could build their own, and then the families would vote on the winner. As the administrative staff, we usually judged these kinds of games, so we rarely participated. To say that we were excited is an understatement. Meetings were had. Blueprints were made. Supplies were purchased. And on the prescribed day and time, the three of us met in my office to build Rapunzel's tower.

Getting Creative

As a team, Jacque, Liz, and I worked well together. But now the pressure was on. Our goal was to have a four-story tower with a roof and decorations in one hour. Graham crackers needed to be stabilized and glued with icing before the next layer was applied. As soon as we held one in place, another one fell over. Our original plan was to build each level separately then combine them when they dried. The plan that we had at the beginning, with meticulously drawn blueprints, was quickly abandoned as our graham crackers crumbled and collapsed. Having no previous experience and expecting this construction to go roughly like a house of cards, we were forced to regroup several times. Our combined years of teaching experience had taught us all how to make fun and interesting toys from water bottles, diaper wipe tubs, sandwich bags, and whatever else we could find. We were not deterred by a few broken graham crackers. We just needed to invest a little creativity.

Two of us rummaged through cabinets and drawers for anything useful. Paper clips, coffee mugs, rubber bands, and rulers were piled on the desk. We crafted an improvised miniature scaffold to stabilize our growing tower. Rapunzel's tower rose slowly but surely, secured by the tiny scaffold until the last of the gumdrop windows were dried.

I had a picture of the three of us with our one-hour Rapunzel's tower in my office until I retired. It was an experience that the three of us cherished. Aside from a fun break from work, we found that the gingerbread tower became a reference point for us during hard times. Getting ready for an inspection? "It's not like we're building a four-story gingerbread house in an hour. This is nothing." Nothing brought that afternoon to the forefront like the time when 20% of our teachers were out sick with the flu. Like we did with the gingerbread house, we made a plan and then threw it away as the severity of the situation set in. We made a new plan, and when that didn't work, we looked at what our stabilizing forces were. Who was willing to switch their lunch earlier or later, who was willing to swap an off day today for another off day later in the week, and other things? We made it through. It's nothing but a gingerbread house.

All of those new things have another interesting effect on us. They help us get out of our creative heads. They help put the brakes on the self-doubt, the imposter syndrome, the I can't do this. That's an important step in the creative process—whether you're trying to figure out how to build a gingerbread house or whether you're trying to figure out a massive staffing shortage. You have to know you can do it. That's hard to do if you haven't already solved that problem. The more new things you do, the more successes you'll have. You'll have a lot more practice with quieting those voices in your head that question whether you can do this thing. You don't have to fight yourself anymore, and now you can turn your attention to the real enemy—the problem.

This shift moves you from self-doubt to idea doubt. Now you're confident that you can do the job. You just need to make sure your idea is the right one for the problem. The shift from self-doubt to idea doubt is important. It puts your ego on the sidelines. It makes it harder to make value judgments about yourself if something doesn't work. Now it's the idea that's the problem. If it doesn't work, we move on to plan B. It's the very definition of Thomas Edison's quote, "I haven't failed. I've just found 10,000 ways that don't work."

One of my favorite examples of this was the Painting with Pinot class that Stephanie and I went to. Me? I was full of self-doubt. I did not paint. I did not craft. I desperately wanted to be one of those women with cute handmade crafty things displayed on their walls "oh, that? That took me an hour or so last weekend in between my son's three baseball games." My previous attempts at crafting had resulted in child-like lopsided constructions consigned to my basement. I really wanted to make this sign.

In the back of the class was an incredulous woman who was there with friends. Her game was idea doubt. She was game for the painting, more game for the wine, and was pretty clear about her artistic level. I liked her immediately.

Getting Creative

The project for our class was to transform wooden pallets into Thanksgiving signs. The model had a brown background with "Give Thanks" in pretty script surrounded by an assortment of warm autumn leaves. The instructor was spunky, if not overly optimistic. She gave us a variety of paint brushes, paints, and water. She patiently doled out instructions and demonstrated flawless technique. Mine smeared. Why did mine smear? Hers didn't smear. Why did mine smear? I looked at Stephanie's project on the easel next to mine. Like the instructor, Stephanie's had no smears. Self-doubt took a step forward, so I took a drink of wine. The teacher moved on to leaves, demonstrating the "easy way" to do it. My first attempt looked like a butchered handprint. Self-doubt was now leaning over my shoulder, pointing. Stephanie's looked identical to the teachers.

"How are you doing that?" I asked her.

"Oh, it's just like this," Stephanie replied and demonstrated the same thing that the teacher had done.

"Dude. Yours doesn't look like that." Self-doubt snorted. My wine glass was empty, and I heard a rumor that there was vodka. I went in search. About this time, the aforementioned woman in the back of the class shouted, "THAT'S THE EASY WAY?!" and let out a loud cackle. As I walked back from the bar with my vodka soda, the woman was

Getting Creative

painting her entire board with a thick coating of orange paint. She picked up a fat paintbrush, painted FUCK THIS SHIT over the orange, and grabbed a nearby bottle of wine. The problem wasn't her; it was this project that was clearly not at the skill level advertised. She spent the rest of the class with that bottle of wine giggling. That woman was officially my hero. I stood next to her in the after-class photo—me with my lopsided handprint leaves, and her with her FUCK THIS SHIT sign.

What that class taught me is to not waste my time trying to make a door out of a wall. A lot of times, if you take a moment and look around, you can find a ladder. You are bigger than one idea. When that one doesn't work, you need to sit still long enough to figure out what to do next. And that can be uncomfortable. You are what give your ideas life and make them special. At the end of the day, though, it's okay to let it go and try something else if something's not working. Remember that

Getting Creative

just because something is solving a problem now doesn't mean it's the best solution or that it can't be improved.

Creativity is an interesting animal. We often think of it as it relates to the arts. And that's just a myth. As I said at the beginning, aside from some photos I'm pretty proud of, I don't consider myself traditionally creative. However, I do think I'm insanely creative in a lot of ways. How do you even find 250 new things to do (mostly) near your home and not be creative? How do you teach yoga to kids and people with chronic pain and not be creative enough to figure out how to make it work for their bodies? How do you live through 2020 with a small business still intact and not be creative? I may not be Picasso, but I own every ounce of my creativity, and you should too.

How do we find it? The same way we've done everything, Pinky. Nice and small. The big lie about creativity is that you have to be on display for it to work. Being an extrovert is handy for success in the arts, but that's about it. Allow yourself time for small creative new things that may lead to bigger creative new things and seek these things out intentionally. If you're not ready to jump into tap dancing, there's no rush. Maybe take in a musical or a concert with unfamiliar music first. Think about a costume party for Halloween. One of my creative new things was our first couple's costume. If you think that doesn't teach you some negotiating, you've never had to discuss if you should be pirates or Alice and Wonderland with your spouse.

Creativity might get harder to find when you're an adult. It's been pushed down so far into the "right" flowers and quieted for "too noisy" that we get the message that to be successful is to conform. We're not allowed to be princesses and superheroes and mummies anymore, and that's a real shame. I know no adults who are jazzed about adulting. When we become adults, there are a lot of rules and roles that we need to follow. Tiaras aren't part of your dress code, and people look at you funny when you talk to your imaginary friends. We have jobs to go to, and they have rules, and policies, and handbooks. We have neighborhood associations that have rules and charters. We have clubs and associations, each with different expectations and policies. Even our friends have expectations. Don't throw up on your friends' shoes. I mean, that's just common courtesy.

But those princesses and superheroes and mummies are still there, waiting to get out. The need to make your mark is still there—although it looks different now. Instead of drawing on your wall, you're drawing on a much bigger scale. It doesn't matter if you're figuring out how to wire a new building, teach boisterous six-year-olds, or how to seat everyone at dinner rush on a Friday night. It might be figuring out how to squeeze new soccer shoes into an already stretched budget. Or it may be putting paint on a canvas in a way that you've never done before.

Creativity is your superpower. You haven't lost your cape. It's just invisible. And it's time to pull it back out.

Getting Creative

FINDING YOUR JOY

Taking Your Shot, Getting in the Swing and Penalties

I AM NOT AN IMMACULATE HOUSE Mother. My mom was not an Immaculate House Mother. My grandmother, however, was an Immaculate House Mother, and many of my friends are Immaculate House Mothers. I always wanted to be in that club--the club where you could come by at any time during the day and counters were clean, the floors were swept and mopped, and the house was perfectly decorated with perfect pillow chops. Still, I was never going to be in the Immaculate House Mother Club. You could barely get into my house because the entryway was always cluttered with a mountain of

Finding Your Joy

backpacks, violins, trombones, hockey bags, shoes, and work bags. Once you traversed the mountain of backpacks, violins, trombones, hockey bags, shoes, and work bags, you'd move into our kitchen where you'd see a table with someone's project in process, a sink full of dishes leftover after a quick dinner cooked between a fourteen-hour day and leaving for a concert or hockey practice. From the kitchen, you'd enter a living room full of lounging neighborhood kids snacking and playing video games. The floor was constantly littered with video game cases and hadn't seen a vacuum in weeks. Our house was full of slamming doors, baskets of undone laundry, street hockey gear, musical instruments, lots of crumbs, lots of laughter, and very, very tired parents. It was loud, and it had a lot of good-natured arguments, and it was full of joy.

Despite that, whenever I went into an Immaculate House Mother's home, I shrunk a little bit inside. To me, that was the epitome of a successful working mom. Despite the joy that ran throughout my home, the clutter and mess were a constant reminder of how I was doing it wrong--how I wasn't measuring up. So I read articles on how to get organized. I read books on time management. I visited websites about how to get your kids to help clean up. Apparently, the secret to that was to give each of them a little box of index cards with their chores listed individually on each one. My kids were incredulous about it, and the whole system fell apart one particularly busy couple of weeks of concerts, tournaments, and a flu epidemic at our school.

After a while, I was exhausted from trying. Nothing worked. I never got my membership card to the Immaculate Mother's Club.

Now here I sit. Some nine or so years later, looking at my sticky floor, and my dusty furniture, and my pillows scattered across the floor (it's a never-ending battle--only the dog and me like the throw pillows on the couch). And I'm here to tell you the amount of time I wasted wishing I could be a part of the Immaculate Mother's Club was not worth it. It was not worth the useless stress that I gave myself and my family. It was definitely not worth the precious little time spent in small gaps in our busy lives arguing about if dishes needed to be done at that exact moment. They don't. Trust me on this.

For all of you who feel like you're outsiders to the Immaculate Mother's Club, for all of you who secretly beat yourself up when you go over to someone's perfectly spotless home, with the pillow chops, and listen to their agonized apologies for "how awful the house looks" just know there are far more of us, the real folks, living real, comfortable, and if we let them be--happy lives. I see you. Even if you think no one else does. Wink.

Finding Your Joy

When I decided to become a permanent outsider of Immaculate Mother's Club, I decided to give up comparing that part of myself to other people, and that felt pretty magical. That's when joy started to really make an appearance in my life. "Comparison is the thief of joy." That was one of Theodore Roosevelt's gems. He's not wrong. When you start giving up the comparisons to other people, joy starts to become self-fulfilling for you. You don't have to be at the whim of others to make you happy anymore, and that is a pretty powerful place to be in. When you are the source of your joy, when you know what you want, you can make decisions about what's truly meaningful to you, what's impactful, and what will continue to bring you joy. You slowly start to weed out what doesn't meet the criteria and feed the joy cycle. Your relationships become more meaningful because you know what you want, and you choose them--intentionally, every day. Your work becomes more meaningful because you're no longer working for just a paycheck. Even in a less-than-ideal job, you find moments of joy and fulfillment and ways to make your work connect to your bigger picture. Yes, even working the Taco Bell drive-thru. I can't tell you how many times my bad day has been changed by Tasha at the Taco Bell drive-thru. Never underestimate the impact your joy has on the world.

Joy becomes a self-fulfilling cycle, and one with the power to extend well beyond ourselves. As you begin to feel more joy from the new things you do in your life, the more you want to find that feeling. You begin to keep your eyes open for places to find that feeling, and the things that get in the way of that feeling begin to slowly fall away. Much like ocean waves crashing into the shore, joy begins to edge closer and closer to you. Every time it retreats, joy pulls back, regroups, and comes back stronger.

On my first trip to Mexico, I woke up early and wandered out to the beach by myself to watch the sunrise. As the sun began to rise over the horizon, the tide started to roll in. I was captivated--waves starting deep in the ocean, rolling forward over themselves until they crashed against the sand and lapped gently at my toes.

With its crashing waves and never-ending horizon, the ocean is so different from our well-defined Midwestern lakes and ponds. Our lakes and ponds are perfectly suited for skipping stones, turtles, and lazy afternoons. Our lakes and ponds that, without fresh water, new life, become murky, smelly, and dank. This is where our malaise lives--our stuckness. In these places where we let ourselves stay small and stop taking chances. When we can begin to look toward the horizon--to move into the waves and enjoy the vibrancy of our joy, we begin to experience the possibilities of our power.

When we think about the things that keep us small, we don't often think about the baggage that other people have given us to borrow. We all have it, and the best thing that we can do is be aware of it. Do you avoid a restaurant because a friend had a bad experience there? Did you become a lawyer like your dad even though you wanted to be a chef in your heart of hearts? Look, the idea of baggage sounds bad, and sometimes it is. But most of the time, those bags are given to us out of genuine love and caring, so your friends aren't thinking of it as baggage. They are thinking of it as loaning your outfits. That's great, as long as you also think they are loaning you cute outfits. They aren't dumping all of their moth-eaten, 70's crappy hand-me-downs on you, along with their hoarder-style boxes of dirty butter tubs and suitcases of mismatched shoes that don't fit. Here's a sample of the borrowed baggage that you may not be aware you are holding:

"Our boss sucks." from conversations from your coworker, who, unbeknownst to you, is close to losing her job.

"People who eat organic are weird," said my father, who never ate anything but blood-red steak and russet potatoes.

"Mexican restaurants aren't clean." said a friend after an unfortunate bathroom incident when he got the green sauce instead of the mild pico de gallo.

Usually, these warnings are well-meaning. Usually, it's because they've either had no experience and have therefore

Finding Your Joy

made up a story to supply the details to save themselves and you, pain and embarrassment, or they've no kidding had a bad experience. They're genuinely trying to protect you. However, you're not them. And it's important to make the distinction between what is their experience and what is your experience because their experiences might just be holding you back.

By the time I was 40, I had never knowingly been in the room with anybody having a gun aside from a police officer. When we were kids, guns were absolutely forbidden in our home in any form. No Nerf guns. No water guns. No rubber band guns, and absolutely no cap guns. We couldn't buy guns at the toy store, we couldn't ask for guns for birthdays, we weren't allowed to have guns of any kind whatsoever. Ralphie's old man had nothing on my dad. There would never be a Red Ryder BB Gun in our house.

I didn't know it then, but my dad's time in Vietnam left him with deep scars. PTSD brought up strong and sometimes barely controlled emotions about guns for him. We also lived in a St Louis City Southside neighborhood, a working-class neighborhood that, while mostly safe, had its fair share of violent crime. Guns for my dad meant very real and living memories. For him, guns meant death. I was absolutely terrified of them.

About a month before Rob and I got married, the seemingly innocuous conversation of whether we have a gun in our house came up over dinner one night. Rob's upbringing had been pretty different than mine. He'd grown up far from the urban center of St. Louis in rural Illinois. While his family never hunted, they had guns in the house, and he was pretty comfortable with firearms. Over a story about hunting on the news, I quipped, "we'll never own a gun." Over a mouthful of spaghetti, he nodded his head said, "of course we're going to have a gun." I looked at him in shock, barely able to speak.

"We are absolutely not getting a gun!" I sputtered. "Guns are how people die!" I could hear my parents' words flowing out of my mouth.

Rob laughed. "Ann, I was raised around guns, and they can be safe if they are stored properly and if you know how to handle them." I was flabbergasted. How could the man that I loved be so wrong? That conversation came up a month before we got married, and it could have ended our relationship.

It didn't, of course. Seeing my abject terror at the thought of a firearm in our home caused Rob to take a breath. It wasn't that important of an issue for him. But he sure saw what I couldn't then, or for a very long time. Heaps of baggage from my parents. Old, stinky margarine bowls full of judgment, ugly sweaters full of their bad memories and trauma, and worn-out, mismatched shoes full of their experiences. I couldn't see any of it, but man, was it heavy.

Decades later, when I started doing the One New Thing Project, Rob saw it as an opportunity to finally offload some of that baggage. He suggested that I take a shooting class as one of my very first new things. He said two very wise things. One, I was holding on to issues that were not mine. The issues were from my parents. And two, the fear that I had was unreasonable because I didn't know anything about guns. Learning about guns, how they worked, and how to handle them might help me understand them a little bit better and feel a little less on edge about them. So, it was with a deep breath and with a good friend that I signed up for a ladies' night shooting class. Collette was one of my oldest friends. She and I grew up in the same South City neighborhood. Her parents had similar feelings towards guns, although for very different reasons. Colette's parents were divorced, and her mom worked long hours. They had very young kids in the house, and it wasn't easy to keep guns out of the hands of curious little ones back in the day. When I told Colette what I wanted to do, she was up for the challenge. We got dressed up in our best Charlie's Angels outfits, with sassy boots, and headed off to the shooting range.

Most of the women in the class with us were there because their partners already had firearms and were basically there to learn how to handle them safely. And then there was Colette and me. The Terrified Two. The instructors gave us what felt like an all-too-brief instruction and safety session before we headed into the range to shoot. I tried to keep the safety information in my mind. *Wait, where was that safety again? Keep the weapon pointed towards the floor.*

We were going to fire three different weapons, the .22, 9mm, and the .38. We each got our own instructor. Mine was an elderly man who was a whole foot shorter than my five-foot two-inch frame. That gave me a certain kind of comfort. He was patient and kind and didn't laugh at me when I picked up the .22 with my hands shaking so violently that the bullet was just as likely to go into the floor of the range as it was to go anywhere near the target. My instructor reached up and placed his hands gently on my shoulders and said, "girl, you got to breathe."

I took a deep breath in and let it out slowly. I followed his careful instructions to look down the sight. When I was ready, he said, "go ahead." And I squeezed the trigger. Next to me, I heard Colette do the same. Colette squealed. She had hit the outer rings of the target. I did not. But I at least hit the target. Collette did a little dance. She looked at mine with excitement. "Ann! Oh my gosh! You did it!!" Yes, I had. I had shot my first gun. I hit the target. With that first shot, I could feel a lifetime's worth of weight drop to the floor. I was ok. No one around me was hurt. I was surprised at how much fun I had shooting at the target. It was empowering. I felt like a badass. A big smile found its way to my face. My tiny instructor was thrilled. He gave me a few adjustments--aiming my sights slightly higher than where I wanted it to hit, adjusting my stance and grip to get more stability. I pulled again. This time I was fully inside the rings. I was getting better. My instructor beamed with pride. As I made more adjustments, I became more comfortable, and I relaxed more. With a few more tries, I had my first of several bullseyes. I was starting to enjoy myself and found that I was a pretty good shot. I learned several different kinds of guns that night, enough that I can comfortably say that I don't like the .38. My aim is better with a .22, and I like the 9 mm the best. I also learned that even though I had a lot of fun and was pretty good for a first-timer, I'm probably just going to stick with shooting at the gun range. I feel a lot more educated about firearms--enough to know that the world is better off with me not having one in a crisis.

I still have the target from that night. It made a move with us when we left our suburban house and moved into the city. It reminds me that I can do hard things--things that scare me. It also reminds me that I always have people who will help me be brave when I don't always feel that way. The night that Colette and I learned to shoot was monumental for me. I was finally able to lay down the baggage that I had inherited from my parents about guns--to separate their experiences from my own. Even more, I was able to stop handing that baggage over to my kids.

When you give up other people's baggage, suddenly the world seems to expand a little bit. You are no longer weighed down. You're a lot lighter, and you can start to give yourself permission to do bigger and bigger things. You can think about how you want to show up in the world--how do you want to look? How do you want to feel?

I know of what I speak. I was the person that hid in the shadows. That was kind of my thing. Don't make waves. Please as many people as you can. Dress the part. People who know me now are skeptical about that. I have curly purple hair. My favorite outfit is a blue retro polka dot shirt dress with maroon Chuck Taylor's--not what you'd expect the mom of a 24 and a 22-year-old to look like. Back in the day, there was a show called What Not to Wear. Two perky hosts would jump out and sabotage people like me for my fashion choices. There was a time that I watched that show obsessively. I hung on their every word, all of their advice so that I fit in—so that I dressed in a way that "fit my body" and wasn't "too young." Now, to be honest, I just don't care. I wear what I love, purple hair and all. It makes me much happier, and that makes me want to make the world happier. I went into a Chipotle on a college campus not long ago. I got no less than three compliments from students on that polka dot dress/Chuck Taylor's combo, so I feel pretty validated. I'm no fashionista, but one of the ways to find your joy and give yourself permission to be you is to wear what you want, listen to the music that you want, and eat the food that feeds your soul, calories, and carbs be damned.

Give yourself permission to express yourself. Let yourself take up space. Live out loud. Give yourself permission to be big--whatever that means to you. You do not have to dance on a bar if that's not your thing. If being big for you means trying a new recipe, that's what being big is for you. One of my very favorite stories about being big isn't even about me. It's about a woman whose name I never learned but whom I'll call Sylvia.

A local yoga group arranged a circus play day to give the public a chance to learn to fly on a trapeze. As soon as I found out about that, I was in. I mean, how often do you get the chance to fly on a trapeze? It was incredible. You climbed all the way up to the top of the twisty rope ladder to stand on top of the tiny platform. You learned to catch the trapeze and then jump off the platform, holding onto the trapeze. You learned to fall onto the giant net and how to roll off the edge. Then, if you wanted, you could learn to hang upside down from the trapeze, swinging out and stretching your arms behind you for a professional to grab your wrists. At that point, you'd release your knees from your trapeze and swing, suspended from the performer's arms until they released you into the net. It was one of the absolute coolest things I've ever done in my life. But as I said, this one's not about me. It's about Sylvia.

There were about 20 or so of us at the circus play day. We were separated into groups to learn the different skills like grabbing the trapeze on the ground and rolling off the net. Sylvia continued to hang back at the edge of the group. The instructors announced that it was time to try our skills on the real trapeze and net. We took turns navigating the twisty rope ladder up to the platform, then grabbing the trapeze, swinging, then falling on the net and rolling off. Ladder, platform, swing, net. One right after the other. Then it was Sylvia's turn. She climbed the rope ladder, twisting and turning. She reached the platform and let out a massive cheer. "I DID IT! I DID IT! I DID IT!" She shouted with a firm grip on the platform's cable. Then she turned around and made a tentative journey back down the ladder, twisting and turning all the way. All 20 of us erupted in applause.

Sylvia's go big moment wasn't flying on a trapeze. Sylvia was afraid of heights. When she saw the circus play date, her only goal was to climb that rope ladder to the platform. That was it. That was her big moment. For other people in our group, it was to swing on the trapeze and fall on the net. For others, it was to do the full catch and release. Your first step to being big is whatever makes sense for you. Your first step might begin tentatively and then turn into a bold move, and then suddenly, it becomes a leap of faith. And that leap of faith becomes something magical. When you start to let go of your baggage, whether it's fears or preconceived notions about how you should dress or act or what you should do in your job, you get unstuck and break down the real and imagined barriers. That's when more things become possible. That's when you start to connect with your joy and your dreams. That begins a cycle that continues to feed on itself. You're filling your bucket without relying on anyone else. You begin to consciously choose things in your life that make sense, rather than passively allowing things that happen to wander in and never leave. Your life begins to feel alive again.

As you consciously choose the things you want in your life, you start to notice the things that don't quite belong there anymore--the things that are slowly but surely getting edged out by your aliveness. They begin to make you feel tight. Constrained. Restricted.

It's a bit like tending a garden. You begin to add in the nutrients, the sunlight, the water, and the good dirt, the peat moss to keep your plants alive, healthy and thriving. You begin to notice the insidious weeds that creep in, threatening to take over, squeezing outgrowth. And so, you start to choose things with intention. You take notice of your champions. You recognize the subtle joy thieves. And you feed the ones that feed you while removing yourself from those that stagnate you.

When you begin to live a life of intention and seek out joy, you begin to step into your power. You're no longer a passenger in your life. You recognize and start to create circumstances yourself that will continue to reinforce your joy. The moments that you spend with your friends and family are all that much more powerful because you're not there by default. You're making a conscious decision to be with them-- to enjoy them and to enjoy those moments. You've determined that they are your champions, and you're theirs. Trust me when I say that you will laugh more with your friends and family when you do this. Until your cheeks hurt. You'll argue more, as well. Because your champions aren't easy on you. They want the best for you, and that doesn't mean letting you off easy. But it's the kind of arguing that you love them for, not the kind that you cry into your pillow afterward, wondering why you keep doing this.

It slowly becomes apparent who around you helps move that forward, who isn't--who is your water and sunshine, and who are your weeds. Pull your weeds. Keep your water and sunshine. They will feed your soul. My biggest champions are my family. My kids are older now, and so we get to have deep and meaningful conversations. Because I don't have to rely on them to constantly fill my bucket, I can be completely present in each and every moment with them--in every laugh, in every argument, in every story, without hoping that they will somehow fill some gaping need for me. Moments like what will likely be our last family vacation together for a while.

It is no small feat trying to coordinate the schedules of four adults with relationships and wildly different work schedules. To say it's complicated is wildly understating it. So that's why in 2019, we offered Alex and Ryan the option of going on a family trip rather than a traditional big Christmas. Rob and I gave them a budget and then left the details of the destination and activities up to them. After tossing around a few ideas-- Toronto, a beach, a cruise, Toronto. They finally settled on a four-day trip to Washington D.C., with a train trip to New York squeezed in. Ryan arranged for a day of lobbying with our Congressional delegation in D.C. and a Capitol tour. That was his idea of fun activities. While we were there, Alex and I stopped in a presidential candidate's office, and they gave us yogurt. Random, I know, but it's true.

Alex found a swanky hotel near Trinity Church in New York to geek out about Hamilton. That was her idea of fun activities. We also planned to see the St. Louis Blues play the New York Rangers at Madison Square Garden. We went to tour Rockefeller Plaza and got a hot tip that tours of Madison Square Garden were going to be starting soon. After some serious sprinting and a lucky subway, we got some good timing and made the tour. That made for some great moments when our family got to go down to ice level and sit in the penalty box. So many history-making moments had happened on this floor, but for Alex and Ryan, they only cared about one. The 1980 Miracle on Ice Olympic Hockey Team played the Soviets here. They lost. Badly. By like nine goals. That game was the beginning of transforming a group of rival college hockey players into a team that would unite a nation. The Disney movie the team inspired would become a mainstay on every hockey tournament trip we went on for nearly a decade.

Near the end of our tour, we were led to the edge of the ice. There was visible awe on the faces of both of my grown children. Standing in the open doors where the Zamboni enters the rink, we looked up at the entire arena, massive in its scale. You could almost hear the crowds cheering. Then our tour guide asked if any of us would like to sit in the penalty box. Alex and Ryan quickly stepped to the front of the line. We walked slowly through the seats into the penalty box. Ryan looked up at the massive scoreboard with a huge grin on his face. Alex looked at me and said, "Mike Eruzione sat right there."

You don't have to know that Mike Eruzione was a captain of that 1980 USA hockey team to know how special that moment was for us. You don't have to know anything about hockey to know that we would remember that moment, of being in that place together, for the rest of our lives. It was all the more special because touring Madison Square Garden wasn't even on our list of things to do. Had we not bumped into a random couple at Rockefeller Center wearing St. Louis Blues jerseys and struck up a conversation with them, we never would have known when the tours for Madison Square Garden were happening. We wouldn't have looked up tour times at that exact moment, and we wouldn't have made the last tour of the day-- the only one we could fit into our trip. That moment of being aware of opportunities for new things gave us what our family has determined to be the favorite new thing our family has done together.

When all of these things come together--recognizing and giving up the things that keep you constrained, allowing yourself to take up space, take chances, be big, live with intention, and have the right people in your corner, you become acutely aware of opportunities around you. You give yourself permission to take advantage of those new things--to try them and to fail. And the power that comes with that is undeniable.

Trying over 250 new things didn't magically take away all of my problems. I didn't suddenly become a Zen, all-knowing guru who has access to all of the mysteries of the universe. I still have a short temper at times. I still struggle with a life-altering chronic illness, depression, anxiety, and PTSD. I still wake up with nightmares a lot. But here's what did change. I gave up forever the need to a part of the Immaculate Mothers Club. The tidiness of my house, or how I was doing as a mom, or at work, or as a wife, no longer had to fill the gaping holes that sometimes show up with anxiety or when my illness rears its head for weeks at a time.

Finding Your Joy

I have many things in my tool belt, learned from many, many new things, to help. I've got a pretty good track record of not just surviving hard things but of doing them with grace and humor. I have good people around me. And that helps me remember that whatever is happening right now is just a thing that's happening for the moment. It won't be here forever, even if it feels like it right now. And with that, you can pretty much take on the world. You don't need a clean house for that. And even if your kids aren't picking up your dusting skills, they are absolutely picking up your take on the world skills. I'd argue that's a lot more impressive.

Finding Your Joy

PASSING IT ON   11

Captain Kirk, Ropes, and Big Words

"I'M IN A TWITTER FEUD WITH WILLIAM Shatner, so that's how my day's going." That's a text that's going to get your attention. Ryan sent that to me one Thursday afternoon. I stared at it for a full minute. He was in college by now, and he never texted unless it was to tell us he was coming home for the weekend. So when I tell you that getting a text from my son saying he was in a Twitter feud with William Shatner was the very last thing I expected, I'm not exaggerating. But here it was.

Over the previous half dozen years or so, Ryan and Alex had gone along with many of the new things that I'd tried. They'd both begun to embrace our family motto of

#makestories. That led to something that none of us anticipated. A Twitter Feud with William Shatner to defend Autistic people.

Shatner, who has a pet Autism advocacy organization that he supports, tweeted some information related to Autism that wasn't accurate. Another user, who was Autistic, replied with some accurate information. Shatner responded harshly, and that's when Ryan stepped in. He's not about sitting back and letting someone get bullied, especially when that someone is a celebrity bullying an Autistic person. Ryan suggested a few other organizations to take a look at. Alex provided a couple of great articles that she and Ryan had written together on growing up Autistic and how the most prominent organization in that field doesn't do the best work for Autistic people. Shatner insulted Ryan pretty colorfully, questioned whether he was even Autistic, and then blocked him.

I'm not sure you can ever prepare yourself for the "I just got blocked by Captain Kirk" text. I'll be honest with you; it was a side effect that I had not anticipated when I started doing new things. It is, however, one of my very favorite stories about Ryan. Routine was and continues to be his jam. As he got older, going along with the flow as people were being hurt or pushed around became less ok with him. And a lot of that came from trying new things. Going along with us on those adventures helped to turn him from the little boy that crouched under the table at his aunt's wedding to the man who stands up for people being bullied.

If I had any advice for parents, it would be to start doing new things with their kids when they are young. Alex was well into her teen years when this experiment began, and she loved the idea of trying new stuff. She was also working on a lot of high-pressure stuff at the time. She was in honors classes, playing field hockey in the Olympic Development Program, and playing in an orchestra—not to mention school sports and plays. That meant that there was a lot of pressure for her to do things well all the time. That's a lot for a fifteen-year-old. She needed a release. She needed to know that it was ok to fail, to screw up, how to have fun with disappointment. Had we started this project earlier, she would have had more of those skills. As a mom, I would have been better equipped to help her. But at that point, I was still figuring out how to be ok with failing. I wasn't much help to her.

I'd love to give you tons of examples of things we did when our kids were young, which led them to be amazing risk takers now. When I started trying new things, it was natural for me to involve my family, but they weren't young. They were teenagers when I started the One New Thing Project. The new experiences that I introduced them to felt pretty small, trivial in the scheme of things. Things like taking them from the safe haven of our suburban bubble, with its Applebee's and Red Robin's, into a historic neighborhood in our city's gritty Northside to a tiny soda fountain that dated to 1913. Red Robin's has milkshakes—good milkshakes. But they have nothing on Crown Candy Kitchen. Crown Candy started making their own ice cream in the 1920s, for crying out loud. They've been perfecting milkshakes for generations. They were one of the first to give you your big fancy milkshake glass, topped with whipped cream and a cherry, and the tin filled with the extra milkshake also filled to the top. Those milkshakes were a meal by themselves.

Crown Candy is a small place adorned with plenty of memorabilia that they've collected over their century or so in operation. It always has a crowd, and you almost always wait in a line that extends out onto the sidewalk. We took our kids on a warm spring day. We got our food, ordered some of the made-on-site candy, and headed outside to find a bench.

Alex and Ryan sat with their cousins, munching on hamburgers and slurping their milkshakes. And then they started talking. We talked about Crown Candy and why it was special. What was it about this tiny soda and candy shop that was so special that it became a legend and stayed around for a century, despite the decline of its neighborhood? We talked about the buildings around us, what the neighborhood was like, and what made it unique. That experience, among others, would begin to open their worldview in a pretty interesting way.

I'm extremely proud of all that my kids have accomplished, especially after trying new things. It gave them a lot of good skills and perspectives they wouldn't have had otherwise. Having said that, I wish we had started much, much earlier.

Little kids are hardwired to try new things. They've only been on the planet for a couple of years, so by definition, almost everything they do is new. They explore, they try things, and they try them again. As they grow up, there's less new stuff. Like most of us, kids do things that are comfortable and familiar with—things that we're pretty good at. It helps us get through life pretty efficiently, but it sort of takes the fun and challenges out of it. Unless that is, we intentionally introduce fun and challenge back into their lives.

Passing It On

Although Alex and Ryan missed out on the One New Thing Project when they were young, during their preschool years, they were lucky enough to go with me to the first school that I directed—a place that was completely different than any of their others. While not necessarily a new thing for them (they were two and four at the time), that school made a pretty big impact on their lives.

The first school that I directed was in an economically distressed area of St. Louis. Most of the kids at that school were raised by single parents struggling to escape poverty. My kids were two of four who were not kids of color. Alex and Ryan spent much of their early childhood there, under the caring and expert guidance of the men and women taught there. Our kids learned to discuss race in the way that kids do, with innocence and curiosity. They learned about the celebrations that families share. They were interested that some kids took the bus to school, some walked, and some drove cars. In our neighborhood, everyone drove. They loved the apartments above our school and would wave to the people who lived there. Our neighborhood consisted only of mostly similar single-family homes. Learning that some kids lived in apartments was fascinating. Finding out that a grandparent sometimes lived with them was the cherry on top. It did lead to awkwardly negotiated conversations about why their grandparents couldn't live with us, but we survived. Alex and Ryan are in their early twenties now, and they still have strong relationships with those teachers. They look back at pictures of their time at that school with fond memories.

Long after Alex and Ryan left that early childhood center, I was surprised to see that they gravitated toward diverse friend groups. In elementary school, they were quick to befriend the school's first Muslim students. Alex's ninth birthday party is still known in our family as the "United Nations party." She invited eight girls that required six different pizzas because of their unique dietary needs. A few years later, Ryan got a sportsmanship award at a hockey camp because he became friends with a kid with Down's syndrome. In my teary, very proud mom moment, I asked him why he hung out with that particular kid. Ryan looked at me, puzzled. "I don't know what everyone is making such a big deal about. I just thought he told good jokes."

Having those early experiences with kids from a variety of backgrounds made a big impact. When Alex and Ryan were young, they learned how to intuitively talk about differences. They weren't afraid to do it. They learned that differences were interesting, fascinating, not something to be afraid of. They learned that different perspectives are valuable, which served them not just in being with people but also in many situations. It helped Alex solve problems in her microbiology lab later, and it helped Ryan solve his coding problems in college. That understanding is also what led to Ryan and Alex stepping in when they saw someone bullying an Autistic person online and would also play a big part in them helping heal Ferguson. This place became special to them after spending so much time with my mom and grandma there.

Another thing that led to those pivotal moments for Alex and Ryan was the confidence that their actions would make a difference. That came from a lot of practice. They did a lot of things. And they failed. And we were there to scoop them up, brush them off, and encourage them to try again. They practiced doing new things over and over, trying and failing, trying and succeeding. It was scary for them, no doubt. It was scary for us too. The first time Ryan checked a kid twice his size in a hockey game. Terrifying. The first time that giant kid checked him back? Gut-wrenching. As we went on, Rob and I got more comfortable with our kids taking bigger risks. I'll be honest with you. As a parent, that's not an easy one to swallow. Our first instinct is to jump in and keep our kids safe. I totally became that insane hockey mom on more than one occasion after cheap shots on my kid, even when he did deserve it. We're all human.

Parents, we need to encourage a level of risk-taking with our kids. We need to let them know that we trust them and the decisions that they make. We need to tell them that if they screw up, we'll still be there. We'll still love them, and we'll help them figure it out. We need to encourage them to start with small and relatively safe new and novel things. That helps them build up their confidence and comfort level to feel ok trying more complex and daring things. The more complicated the things your child is trying, the more their brain is working—and that means there's good problem solving and predicting happening. That means your child is starting to think about what has worked in the past, what lessons they've learned, and what they might be able to apply in this situation. Then they start to think about what new strategies they can try. Trying new things, challenging and risky things, encourages creativity. It encourages tenacity. It encourages leadership. It encourages resilience and humor. Yes, humor. It's a good time to learn to laugh at ourselves when the stakes are low.

Don't worry; that doesn't mean that I'm advocating that your kids should jump off the table. But I am advocating that we teach our kids how to learn what it feels like when risk feels right and doesn't. It means that when someone asks them to try something that doesn't feel good, they'll be ok with saying no—because they've had practice.

Encouraging risk-taking in your kids is all about knowing their personalities. Even as little ones, you'll have your watchers, your do-ers, and your planners. It's also ok to respect that your child does not want to do something right now. They may be interested at some point, or maybe never. This game is all about slowly expanding comfort zones, and it doesn't work if we push too hard. Remember, we don't all have the same personalities, and what you find thrilling might terrify your child. Respect that. We got a pretty good look into our kids' personalities when Alex was four and Ryan was two. We were at my brother's house so they could play with my nephew, Matt, who is six weeks younger than Ryan. The kids had been begging for cookies. Exasperated, we finally put the cookies up on top of the refrigerator until after dinner and sent them off to play. The adults went back to playing cards, thankful for a little adult solitude. After some time, my brother's wife commented that the kids were suspiciously good-quiet. As the more experienced parents, Rob and I exchanged looks. Quiet probably meant trouble. We headed into the kitchen, followed by my brother and his wife, to find my two-year-old nephew sitting on top of the refrigerator, handing the cookies down to Ryan, who had climbed onto a counter. Alex was standing next to a chair pushed up to the counter.

"What are you doing?" I asked.

"It was Ryan's idea. Matt's getting the cookies, and I'm supervising." Alex replied.

There you had it. Ryan, the planner. Matt, the do-er, Alex, the supervisor.

I told you that I would not get behind kids climbing up on tables, and I'm not. Our kids got in major trouble for that one. Safety always comes first. We learned to hide the cookies better and not underestimate three motivated toddlers' combined problem-solving abilities. Ryan would never have been the kid on top of the refrigerator. Even then, heights were never his thing, and Alex was always the one who stuck by the rules. Matt, on the other hand, has always been more of a risk-taker. Trying to push Ryan into bigger and bigger risks too fast has backfired on us every single time. Alex always needed context for the new things that we were doing. She loved doing them, but she always fared better when she had an idea of how they fit into her world. Knowing your kids' personalities, and fitting the experiences to them, is critical for them to work—whether they end up being successful or a failure that you need to figure out.

As we grow up, the idea of creatively solving a problem like how you get the cookies from the top of the refrigerator gets drilled down to the one correct answer. Mostly, parents tell us we don't. Taking risks becomes scarier because our ego gets involved. I got in trouble, so I shouldn't climb to the top of the refrigerator again. We get a little better at remembering things and predicting future events. That means if you fail at something, that's kept in your brain and comes up every time you get close to a situation, that's even remotely like that. If I climb to the refrigerator, I'll probably get in trouble again. Plus, I haven't seen the cookies up there since. Better look somewhere else.

Obviously, you may not have had the great experience of finding your kids in the middle of stealing cookies off the top of the refrigerator. Still, my guess is you've seen this or experienced it yourself. Maybe it was always knowing when to avoid your dad in a bad mood. Or always knowing how to get five bucks out of your grandma. Perhaps it was avoiding dodgeball because you weren't super athletic. Maybe it was letting everyone else do the work in the group projects. You start to stick to safer options where you might not look silly, stupid, or incompetent. Where people might not make fun of you. Hello, perfectionism. I missed you.

That's a lot of pressure if you're in, say, middle school or high school, where your peers suddenly become your important reference. Suddenly, you feel like everyone looks better, knows more, is better at everything, and generally has their shit together more than you. I have not yet met one person over eleven who thinks they truly have their shit together for more than 30 straight minutes. At least when we're adults, we have an idea that those "go me!" moments will come back around. Kids don't yet know that.

When it comes to our children taking risks, we send some seriously mixed messages. We want kids to be bold and to go after their dreams. For them, that's not always as easy as it sounds. Think about the courage it takes to try out for teams, plays, scholarships, and what have you. You're telling people exactly what you want most of all and asking other people to judge you. Think about a teenager coming to their parents as transgender. How scary must that be to tell a mom excited to go prom dress shopping with her daughter? What about the star athlete that is depressed? Everyone tells them what a great life they have—how jealous they are. Imagine how terrifying it must be to tell someone that you feel like a fraud—to say to your friends that you think you have it made. The risk for rejection, condescension, gaslighting, and humiliation is huge. It's pretty easy to see why kids stay silent. What if they could learn to let all of that go?

Doing new things is a lot like learning a new language. It's best if you start when you're young because you become more comfortable with the whole idea of it. Taking chances, failing, and figuring it out becomes second nature. But you don't have to start when you're three. Alex and Ryan are proof of that.

Ryan never liked heights. After Ryan had his concussion, he avoided them entirely. His vestibular system, the system that tells your body where it is in space, was knocked offline, so he was prone to serious bouts of vertigo. During his physical therapy, we'd go swing on a playground until he got dizzy. Most days, he'd only go a few seconds, then take just a few steps before coming close to toppling over. It sidelined him from hockey for a year, so in the interim, he picked up tennis. The school tennis team planned a team-building trip to a local zip line course. For Ryan, if he's a part of a team, he does all of the team activities. It didn't matter that this one was 30 feet off the ground, with lots of swinging ropes, and would probably be a big problem for his vestibular issues. He would have to figure out a way to make it work. His idea was to do a practice run with us. He'd be able to get the lay of the land, figure out what areas caused the most problems, and that way, he'd be able to know what help he needed and how to get it.

A week before the tennis team's trip, we made a reservation for the zip line course. We got our safety harnesses, helmets, and safety clips. Instructors led us through clipping in and transferring our safety ropes between stations. Then they wished us good luck and sent us off to the first station. Alex climbed the long rope ladder to the platform, followed by Ryan. They analyzed the rope bridge, figuring out the best way to work through it, then one of them tested their idea. On and on, they went through each increasingly difficult obstacle. Stop. Analyze. Test. Often, they would fail and fall off completely. Hanging there, suspended only by their safety ropes 30 feet above the ground, they'd discuss their options and decide on another idea. Then they'd pull themselves up and try again. Those failures let Ryan go slowly enough to keep his vertigo in check. At the same time, Alex's mind was always at work figuring out how to solve the problem at hand. It allowed her to take a much-needed mental break from the college essays, applications, and relentless AP class requirements. At the end of the day, both Alex and Ryan were able to make the experience work in a way that benefitted them, for what they each needed at that time.

Encouraging our teenagers to take risks makes us feel a little uneasy because we feel like it won't end with family trips to the zip line. I know. You're thinking back to all the stuff you did as a teenager. I did too. I'm going to offer you a different perspective. As adults, we want so much to keep our kids safe that the idea of them taking risks on purpose is scary for us. We did a lot of crazy stuff as kids. We all have "I can't believe I lived through that" moments (most of us figuratively) and things that our parents would have died if they had known about. My guess is they knew about 75% of it and never said anything. How do I know this? Because I knew about 75% of the stuff my kids did. And it's better that I don't know the other 25%.

The tween and teen years are hella hard. You have school. You have extracurriculars. You have dating and heartbreak. You have jerks at school. You have teachers that you don't get along with. All of a sudden, your parents seem like strangers. Guys, it's hard. What if we could equip our young people with the skills to navigate those waters? Trying new things might be just that. I saw that as Alex and Ryan tried more and more new things, they got better at advocating for themselves and others. They were ok with being at a party and telling people that no, they didn't want to drink because they just didn't feel like it. They were ok with ending friendships because they were becoming toxic. I saw them tell people, "I'm not going to let you treat me this way." Guys, I was over 40 and hadn't mastered that.

There isn't much research about the positive effects of trying new and novel things in childhood and adolescence. Still, based on what I've seen with my kids and their friends, I'm convinced that it has a powerful effect. It opens possibilities. It shows you how powerful you are. And that is an incredible combination.

In the winter of 2016-2017, Alex was in her junior year of college studying microbiology in a tiny rural town in Illinois. We were witnessing a backlash against science, academics, and research. Alarmed by what she was seeing, Alex was moved to action. She contacted organizers of the National March for Science. Affiliate marches were planned to occur not just around the United States but around the world. Still, no one had yet stepped up to organize an event in St. Louis. Alex decided to take it on. She spent the next six months working with two strangers to build a diverse board to lead the St. Louis March for Science. She helped to create committees, organize permits, staging, and speakers for the program. She drove four hours each way from her campus to St. Louis each week to meet with the team and coordinate with other organizers from around the world. She contacted a remarkable keynote speaker and organized a social media campaign that resulted in the third-largest March for Science in the country. On that April morning, we followed her as she and the other organizers led over 20,000 people to the Arch grounds. Then one of the teachers from her first preschool stood next to me as we watched her give the opening address as a sea of people cheered her on.

Alex wasn't always that person. She was more outgoing and more of a risk-taker than her brother was, but that didn't mean she wanted to try everything. One time I had to bribe her to spend the weekend at her grandparents' house when she was eight. When I talked to her on the phone one night, she lowered her voice and said, "I don't like it here. You need to come and pick me up right now. Bring me chicken nuggets." Apparently, Grandma had tried to make chicken nuggets from scratch that she assured Alex were way better than McDonald's. For an eight-year-old, nothing was better than McDonald's chicken nuggets, and Grandma's didn't come with a toy.

She grew into the person who would speak to 20,000 people over many years. Ryan, too, grew into his own. And so did Rob and me. Trying new things for us and encouraging Alex and Ryan to try their own new things gave us a chance to get used to our kids taking chances and letting them handle the rough times on their own, mom and dad close enough to support, but not close enough to take over. It was a lot like putting your toes in a frigid swimming pool, slowly warming up to everything as we all got comfortable. All of us trying things out—Alex and Ryan trying their new things, and Rob and I trying to not solve everything when they failed.

When Alex was a senior in high school, she was elected to give the senior night address to her graduating class. She spoke about the importance of trying new things. She talked about the many new things she had done, large and small—everything from trying different flavored potato chips to her orchestra trip to New York. She talked about how although the next phase of her life at college was many things, uncertain, scary, and exhilarating, she felt confident to take it on because it was just one more new thing at the end of the day. She encouraged her classmates to continue to take chances, try new things, and enjoy the ride. She said that, at the end of the day, whether we fail or succeed, life is all about the stories we make. And we've made some pretty incredible ones.

MARCH FOR SCIENCE
SAINT LOUIS
Real People, Real Science.
18th St

Passing It On

EPILOGUE

One New Thing #287:
Wrote A Book

WHEN MY GRANDFATHER WAS DYING, I sat by his side every night talking with him, drinking in his stories. My grandfather was an engineer at McDonnell Douglas, now Boeing. He helped design the F-15 that was retired a few years ago. He was on a first-name basis with the company CEO. He gave up wearing a tie early, and once when called into a meeting with heavy hitters, he had to borrow one from my uncle because all of his smacked of the decade before. Lying on a hospital bed late at night, Grandpa told me stories about vacationing with friends in the Ozarks. They would take their boat out at night, have a few cocktails, and moon the other boats. I learned more about my grandfather during those days than I had in my entire life up until that point.

One night, in between sharing stories, he looked me dead in the eye and said, "You work too hard. You need to relax." It

Epilogue

caught me by surprise at the time. I think about that a lot. My grandfather, a skilled engineer, working on military aircraft, ditching his ties long before business casual was an accepted practice. My grandparents and their friends, whom I knew only in their later years as my aunts and uncles with wrinkles, pearls, and canes, in their prime laughing and drinking and dropping their pants on a boat. We have a huge Irish Catholic Family, and I'm the only one that got that story.

So that's why in May of 2020, I finally sat down to do this project. As I waited out COVID, isolated in the bedroom of our 1890's south St Louis house, I was finally starting to feel a little better, but I still had a lingering cough. We were still figuring COVID out then, and we didn't know that the cough would hang on for a while—especially for us asthmatics. My doctor told me that I had to be free of all symptoms for 36 hours before coming back in contact with my family, so that isolation just kept stretching out.

The project that I was settling in for was something I've wanted to do for a very long time--cataloging all of the new things that I've done, collecting all of the stories. I searched through old Facebook posts, pictures, a starter blog on Tumblr and pulling all of them together. Each year started to come together--small things, big things, massive achievements, and epic fails. As I pulled together threads of my new things, my family and I shared stories about them as they sat on the steps leading to our bedroom. I sat on the windowsill in my room—all of us wearing masks, 20 feet apart. It gave us something to laugh about, a way to stay connected during those long weeks apart.

As I painstakingly pulled together all of those memories and stories, as my family retold them, I wanted to capture every moment—to make sure that none of it was forgotten. I wanted to make sure that all of the things that I did don't end up, like my grandfather's stories, in one person's hands.

Those conversations with my grandfather happened a full ten years before I started thinking about doing new things. But it occurred to me more than once during my project how similar my friends and I were to my grandparents and their friends. We never mooned anyone on a boat in the Ozarks. Still, once I freed myself from other people's expectations, I started to live more, laugh more, and adventure more.

Our family is full of storytellers. We recount our experiences over and over again, in vivid detail. It's how I found out the real story about how Alex broke her arm when she was ten—a secret kept between brother and sister for over a decade about how they were playing on an off-limit dilapidated hammock in our backyard. It's how our kids know the story of their mother throwing up on our first date after one and a half Bartles and James wine coolers.

Epilogue

When I was able to step back and see the full scope of my project, I realized that my journey, which felt like an epic adventure of self-discovery, was also about the stories and memories that I shared with others. Memories and stories are what bind us together. The night that we made chocolate bowls from Pinterest, and they exploded, leaving chocolate all over the kitchen ceiling. The bird-sized grasshopper that pinned itself to my dress in Mexico. Alex and Ryan outsmarting senators. It makes me happy that my new things not only gave me something, but they also have given the people in my life a lot of joy.

When I started the One New Thing Project, I had a lot going for me, but I felt like I was getting it all wrong. I wasn't connected with a lot in my life because I could only see where other people were doing it right, and I was missing the mark. I don't feel that way anymore. I don't see where I do not measure up to someone else's clean house or perfect dinners. Instead, I see strong people who are struggling like I am and who care about different things. I was finally able to release that and focus on what's important to me—the people in my world. I'm so grateful for how this project has brought me closer to the people that I love most in the world. We have more memories together. We know where each other is strong and how to support each other. And we have stories that belong to us—that no one can take from us.

Epilogue

I never thought I'd write a book about this. If there's one thing that I've learned from my One New Thing Project, it's that we don't do things in a vacuum. What I thought was a solitary self-care project was and is a very real group effort. I didn't realize at the time the effect the new things were having on me—I couldn't until I pulled back and looked at all of them together. But the people around me did. They saw me laugh more. They saw me speak up more. They saw me give up the "we've always done it this way." They were proud of me when I was unsure. They encouraged me to keep going when I didn't know if I could. They reminded me that I could do hard things. That was monumental because even though I was doing new stuff, I made a lot of big changes. To be honest, I didn't know if they'd all pan out. When you leave the only career you've done for 30 years with no safety net, that's a scary proposition. The people around me continually reminded me to enjoy this new thing—the uncertainty, the newness, the failures, and every one of the successes.

As I started compiling my experiences, I started to see the full impact of this project. There was no denying that I was a different person from the first time I tasted that mooncake almost a decade before. I won't pretend that it's been an easy journey. It hasn't cured my illness, and it hasn't cured my PTSD.

Epilogue

But they no longer define me. There is incredible joy even in dark moments.

I'll be honest. When I started the One New Thing Project, I never thought I'd end up here. When I started, I thought I'd be lucky to do enough new things to get me through the year—I'd never finished a New Year's Resolution so that by itself would have been a big deal for me. Most of the people around me thought what I was trying to do was interesting. Still, given my track record for following through on things and my ability to go against the grain, a lot of them thought that I wasn't going to do this One New Thing-thing for very long. Secretly, I agreed with them.

I'm not sure when that changed. Somewhere between playing with hot glass to make a lopsided paperweight and making sushi with my kids, I started to see myself differently. I started to see all of the things that I was capable of, not the places I let people down and failed. The people around me, who at the beginning treated my New Year's Resolution with mild curiosity, became my biggest supporters. They started asking what my next thing was. As the days of the month ticked by and they saw no posts about new things, they started sending me ideas. They held my courage when I couldn't hold it on my own.

The more people I shared this with, the more people said, "I know *exactly* how you felt. That's me." And that's when I decided to take on the scary proposition of sharing my One

New Thing Project with the big bad world—to share New Thing #287, this book, with you in hopes that you know that in those moments of doubt, there are a lot of people rooting for you.

With this book, my goal with this project is to open the door for you. For those of you who feel alone in a crowded room. For those of you who feel like your house is never clean enough. For those of you who worry that your kids will get hurt, go to the wrong party, or make the wrong decisions. For those of you who feel like your job or relationship just doesn't fit anymore. I want you to know that even though it feels like you are all by yourself, you're not. There are thousands of us—millions, even, that are right there with you. We're quiet in book clubs and P.T.A. meetings and soccer practices, quietly contemplating why everyone else has their stuff together, and we don't. Maybe next time you make eye contact with someone in one of those situations, give a wink. They're probably thinking the same thing you are.

I want you to know that you don't have to feel like that. You can find yourself again. We are a strong and inspired community. We are the people who lean on each other and inspire each other. We pick each other up, dust each other off, and remind each other just how magnificent we are. The people who are embarking on this journey together are finding new

Epilogue

things to do, sharing their ideas, and doing new things together, even in the worst pandemic we've seen in over a century.

Your One New Thing Project is entirely yours—something that will evolve into a deeply personal connection with what inspires you, what no longer serves you, and how to meaningfully interact with your world and the people in it. There are no boundaries on what you can do. Be as small as you want or as big as your heart desires. The choice is up to you.

Go make your stories.

Made in the USA
Monee, IL
03 August 2021